# contents

- foreword by stewart lee ... 3
- introduction by steve goldman ... 5
- introduction by simon robinson ... 6
- here pussy ... 8
- you are what you eat ... 9
- lothar and friends ... 11
- f f fashion ... 13
- jodelfeest ... 14
- gangsta breaks ... 15
- paint by numbers ... 19
- say cheese ... 23
- f f fashion ... 27
- watercolour challenge ... 30
- leather chamois and spandex studs ... 35
- disco ducks ... 42
- something for the ladies ... 43
- fnar fnar ... 52
- privately pressed ... 53
- classical capers ... 56
- performing seals ... 62
- glam gone wrong ... 64
- diskos diva ... 66
- hash-tag metoo ... 68
- visible flakes ... 71
- primark moment ... 72
- the eyes have it ... 73
- sausage time ... 75
- meh ... 80
- way out west ... 81
- you can't pick your family ... 83
- he's more than just a swear word ... 85
- an apple a day ... 95
- trees talk too ... 96
- joyeux noel ... 99
- seven inch strangeness ... 106
- tragedy ... 108
- laughs with olaf ... 110
- showbands ... 112
- animal farm ... 116
- like a ship on the ocean ... 117
- more disco ducks ... 119
- the eyes have it again ... 122
- yet more disco ducks ... 123
- metal mistakes ... 126
- vox cantoris ... 128
- jazzercise ... 131
- prince jammy ... 134
- lady's fancy ... 135
- face off ... 142
- instrumentally yours ... 147
- break beats ... 149
- motorbikin' ... 150
- pink ... 152
- taboo ... 154
- 80 words per minute ... 156
- dummy piano ... 159
- new faces ... 160
- over wrought iron ... 164
- top hit aus holland ... 166
- is it memorex ... 168
- whipped cream ... 169
- salad days ... 171
- peter's rabbits ... 172
- good time music ... 174
- easy on the eye books ... 178
- credits and acknowledgements ... 180

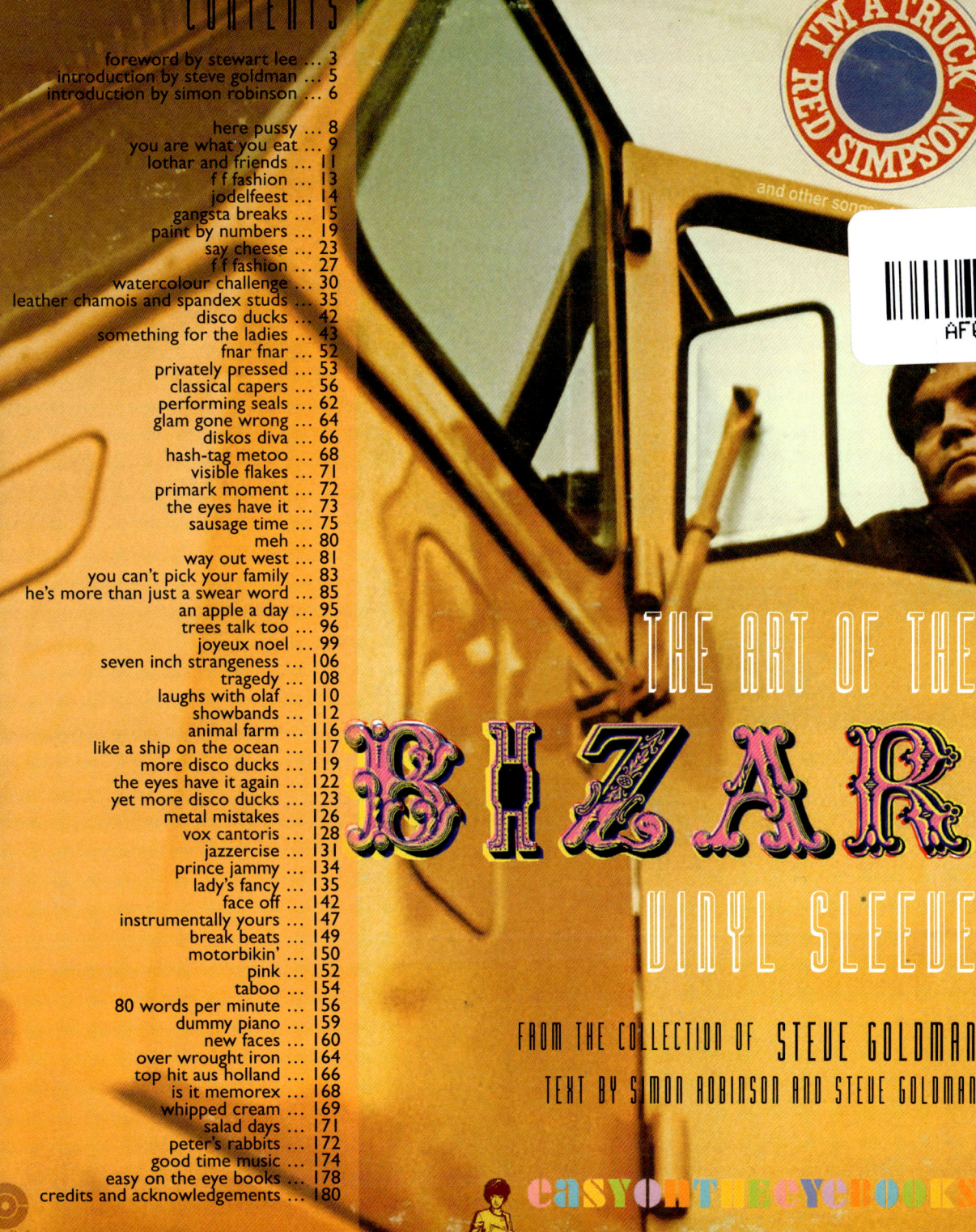

I'M A TRUCK RED SIMPSON and other songs

THE ART OF THE BIZARRE VINYL SLEEVE

FROM THE COLLECTION OF STEVE GOLDMAN
TEXT BY SIMON ROBINSON AND STEVE GOLDMAN

easyontheyebooks

# FOREWORD / STEWART LEE

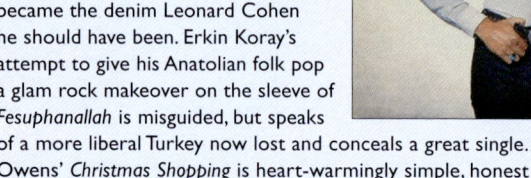

I understand from experience what is funny about The Bizarre Record Sleeve. In the early '90s I used to tour the clubs and colleges as a stand-up comedian, in a little trio with future Tinky Winky actor Dave Thompson, and a spesh-act called Woody Bop Muddy. Woody was formerly known as William Wilding of …And The Native Hipsters, the 1980 indie-hit-makers of *There Goes Concorde Again* fame. If only I'd appreciated his cultural significance back then, I'd have probed him for post-punk insight from service station to service station. But I was young and ignorant.

William had a bit called Record Graveyard, where dressed as a pirate and standing on his own portable desert island, he would hold up a bizarrely sleeved old piece of vinyl to the baying crowd of drunks, play them a section of the record on a battered Dansette, and then, like some crazed maritime Caesar, invite the peasants to 'save it' or 'nail it', the doomed records being hammered to a cruel plank at the centre of the island, festooned with the shattered fragments of other despised vinyl.

Every day, William would strip-mine charity shops for suitably stupid looking records. Copies of *And Then I Change Hands*, a soft rock album the '70s children's TV presenter Mick Robertson [right], rarely survived the show, and he must have destroyed dozens, but I once intervened personally, rushing the stage, to save a copy of Peter Hammill's *In Camera* which was, for no obvious good reason, about to get nailed. As well as a stand-up, I'm a record collector. And thirty years later, *In Camera* is recognised as a lo-fi proto-Goth classic. But where is William Wilding now? He is a successful performance artist and local councillor in Herefordshire. Oh.

I love records and I'm professionally obliged, as a stand-up comedian, to see the funny side of things, and so when they asked me to write a few hundred words introducing The Art Of The Bizarre Record Sleeve I thought it would be fun. But I was wrong. Very wrong. Because somewhere, between Mistral's *You're My Hero* and Glen Daley's *A Hundred Thousand Welcomes* the relentless low quality and relentlessly poor aesthetic choices of the sleeves made me despair of humanity itself. I began to hate mankind for its ineffable and inexcusable shitness, its natural tendency towards ugliness and stupidity, and I thought we deserved everything a vengeful mother nature is currently throwing at us as a species. In the midst of this mess, an explanation of the design tug-of-war that blights and accidentally makes marvellous the sleeve of Lothar And The Hand People's pioneering '68 oddity *Presenting…*, which I own and enjoy non-ironically, was welcome. But otherwise, the organisms that gave the earth Orion's *Reborn* should not be saved. Up to a point kitsch is funny, then it begins to speak of our collective failure to understand true beauty, and makes me feel sickened to my soul. I began to hate this whole project, and specifically the men behind it Steve Goldman, whose collection the book represents, and Simon Robinson, who has corralled it into some kind of shape. But then the homemade metal imagery of Kopperfield's *Tales Untold* and Battleaxe's *Burn This Town* gave me hope. There was something noble about the artists' attempts to reach for something, some feeling of the epic and the transgressive, so clearly beyond them. Then I began to view the subsequent selection of international disco design disasters as somehow heroic, the unwelcome nudity of Herbie Mann, Carlos and Alan Franklin challenging us to reject their essential unprocessed humanity. Neil Diamond's phallically suggestive *Hot August Night* is actually the best sleeve he ever sported, and points to a parallel world in which he became the denim Leonard Cohen he should have been. Erkin Koray's attempt to give his Anatolian folk pop a glam rock makeover on the sleeve of *Fesuphanallah* is misguided, but speaks of a more liberal Turkey now lost and conceals a great single. And Buck Owens' *Christmas Shopping* is heart-warmingly simple, honest and direct. Tommy Ellison's *Let This Be A Lesson To You (Drunk Driver)* has the haunted quality of one of Ithell Colquhoun's surrealist collages.

Elsewhere, disowned images, like the hurried sleeve of Black Sabbath's 1983 effort *Born Again*, which Steve Joule disavowed, and the new and hurriedly withdrawn 1977 doll-in-a-desert sleeve for Deep Purple's eponymous 1968 debut, have, to me, fared rather better than the usual metal cliches. And the collision of functional design and informative titles on a selection of info-albums create accidental unrealised Guided By Voices record titles; *The Fascination of Coins; Plant Problems Answered; Sobriety and Beyond*; and *Actual Business Letters Dictated At Various Speeds*. Idiocy can trump intent. The contemporary space-disco-prog band Henge have put a lot of time and thought into trying to create a visual aesthetic as coherently unhinged as the one Holland's Mistral arrived at without much apparent analysis.

The Swedish flautist Merit Hemmingson's *Gastabud* sleeve suggests pagan fertility ritual, but the album itself, which I felt compelled to investigate, is bland cocktail jazz. Like so many of those featured here, the sonic shapes the sleeves suggest to the viewers' imagination are probably stranger than the actual sounds themselves. Brazilian duo Daduca and Dalvin's anonymously futile 1989 LP *Massa Falida*, for example, is inaccurately served by a techno-pagan sleeve depicting an angel in a mystic triangle emerging from seawater between the two singers, attired in revealing swimwear.

But not every strange looking record is shit. My Uncle Roger left for Canada in the late '60s to become an air steward and escape the British class system,

*Below - Stewart Lee crate digging in Rays Jazz Store at Foyles Charing Cross Road, 2006. PHOTO Gary Carlton*

leaving behind a pile of records many of which, like Herb Alpert's *Whipped Cream and Other Delights* featured here, showcased sleeves of women in stages of undress. My favourite of the discarded nudie vinyl was *Jungle Adventure In Music And Sound*, a 1966 jazz-exotica session overseen by Salvatore Camarata and post-produced with birdsong and ape calls that I defy anyone who hears it to dismiss. Somewhere behind the sleeves catalogued here will be something similarly superb. But that isn't the point of this book.

Instead, treat each record as a visual item in its own right and try to view it through the same lens that has made this woeful world of loss so fascinating to our authors. In showcasing the cheapest and yet most sincere sleeves they can find, Goldman and Robinson are defining an as yet uncategorised new substrata of folk art. Because thirty years ago Steve Goldman saw the sleeve of *Roadstar* by Peter Rabbitt and understood that sometimes the chance meeting of ineptitude, naivete, underfunding, tastelessness and hope can combine to create a whole new surreal and impenetrable artistic statement somehow far greater than the sum of its often stupid parts.

*Stewart Lee, writer/clown, Stoke Newington, September 2023*

We asked Dolly Parton, King Sized Dick and Stewart Lee if they could contribute forewords for the book. Stewart was the only one who replied. We then wondered what one album he might add to this collection; he came back straight away with *I Play The Host* by Alexander Lord Weymouth, a 1974 album produced by Des O'Connor for the 7th Marquess of Bath... O'Connor was a big selling MOR recording act for Pye, and after signing to the label in 1973 (from Columbia, where he'd been since the late 1950s) was credited as a producer on many of his own recordings and for a handful of other artists. According to Bath (as he often signed himself), O'Connor heard him performing a song on the BBC (the Marquess' eccentricities mean he has a long history of media appearances) and got in touch to ask if he had any more material, which of course he had. A lot. O'Connor offered to secure a deal with Pye and to produce, and via his own music publishing company, signed up the rights. Given this usually prompts an artist advance, one doubts he got his investment back.

Pye immediately relegated the album to their budget label Golden Guinea (albums which originally sold for £1.1s. 0d), a sure sign that they didn't see any commercial potential. And even on the cover the Marquess admits that rather than aiming for pop stardom the reason for doing it was to gain some profile for his poetry, in the hopes of finding a publisher.

Promotion came when the Marquess played a track on his Radio 4 Desert Island Discs appearance in 1975 (though Sue Lawley cut it noticeably short) where he was quick to give credit to Bryan Daly's excellent guitar work (Daly is maybe better known for the Postman Pat soundtrack album!) which elevates the otherwise edgy (as being on the edge of unlistenable) performance no end. Engineered by Ray Prickett (probably at the Pye Studios) the record is as directionless as the 7th Marquess's life might suggests it would be.

The cover photograph is a strange contrast between the folksie pose and attire of the Marquess (love the claw band chain...) set against the backdrop of his folksie stately home. It is not credited, suggesting (as does the poorly aligned and cropped transparency) an in-house job.

The album is a rare artifact, copies no longer available even from the Longleat gift shop....

# INTRODUCTION / STEVE GOLDMAN

There's a record (it's in the book, page 172) called *Hand in Hand*. The cover is a colour photo of nine people, forming a circle in a field, hand in hand. Except one of them couldn't make the shoot, so is replaced by a black and white photo of his face, twice the size of everyone else's head, in a frame. I start sniggering the moment I spot it. I've got to add it to my collection.

How did I get here?

Over thirty years ago, in a cut-price basement record shop called Yanks in Manchester, I bought *Roadstar*, an album by Peter Rabbitt, for 10p, simply because it was such an extraordinarily terrible cover. Subsequently I lost it. Then the internet came along: I thought I would try and find a copy. Yet whenever I did a web search, all it came up with were links to Beatrix Potter. But I often thought about the album, and whether I would ever see it again.

Then in 2016, someone told me about Discogs, a site where not only do people contribute to what is now the world's biggest vinyl database, but collectors buy and trade. So I looked there and Peter Rabbitt's album came up for £5 (plus another fiver to have it shipped from Germany). When it arrived it was one of the happiest moments of my life. And that evening, I said to my family, *"You know what? I think I'll start collecting terrible record covers..."*

As the collection grew, I would show them to anyone who came round. One day after *The Nimble Fingers Of Jean Pierre Jumez* cover made an old friend of mine laugh more than I'd ever seen her laugh before, I thought I should try exhibiting these so everyone could enjoy them. Kirklees Council let me have an empty shop window unit to display them in and the public really enjoyed it. So did the media, and their interest allowed me to start showing the collection at other venues and festivals.

I have a few rules. First and foremost, the sleeve has to make me laugh. Second there are plenty of bad album covers which are just sexist / racist / homophobic or plain unpleasant. You won't find any of these in my collection. My favourite bizarre covers are where the concept or context has gone horribly wrong. With the band, artist, photographer, design agency AND record label all letting it pass.

I'm still collecting and, several exhibitions later, people are still laughing. Here's a selection of the 'best', chosen in part from worst sleeve polls I carried out at the shows. I hope they make you laugh as much as they do me.

Steve Goldman

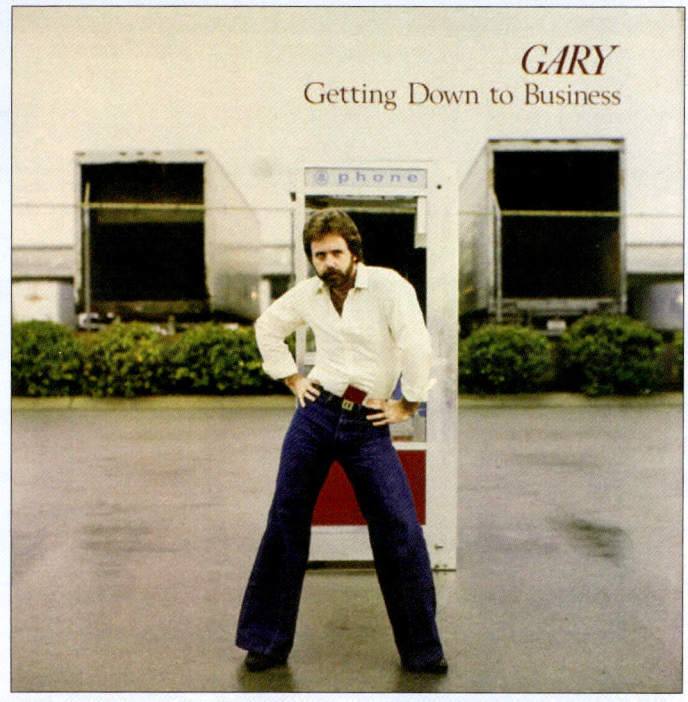

# INTRODUCTION

I am not 100% sure what sparked my lifelong interest in album sleeve art but have a strong memory of being fascinated as a schoolchild by *The Who Sell Out* cover on display in a record shop window in Sheffield. As I began to find my own popular music interests, the packaging and art on underground and progressive rock albums began to generate as much interest for me as the music. Art college beckoned and I got to design my first sleeve for EMI in 1980. It was the quality of the artwork, design, photography and typography which determined my own response to covers, elements which I probably paid far too much attention to when with two friends we founded the CD reissue label RPM in the Nineties. Not for me simply reproducing the rare Joe Meek *I Hear A New World* EP cover on a CD, I had to identify the photo library Meek used for the original cover and secure a print to work from. No wonder we never made much money.

As well as collecting interesting covers myself, some discoveries were so strange and weird that if cheap enough I also picked them up. This came in handy when tasked with packaging a CD of the many chart covers sessions featuring a young Elton John on vox, giving me an excuse to fall back on my growing collection of *Hot Hits* and *Top Of The Pops* albums for 'inspiration'.

So when a couple of years ago Tom Dixon emailed me about a pop-up display of The Worst Record Sleeves in not too far away Huddersfield, I had to investigate. I was moving into publishing with Easy On The Eye Books. Might there be some synergy here, I asked the curator.

Our first sight of Steve Goldman's collection on display was the clincher. We were in fits of laughter for about an hour, a not uncommon reaction he told us. Indeed that is by and large his criteria for the collection, the covers must make him laugh.

Looking at the covers en masse, there was also incredulity and wonder; how had nobody spotted how some of these covers might look to others? Hindsight is of course wonderful but you would have hoped someone might have seen the pitfalls in enough time to come up with something better. But then we wouldn't have this book…

It was also fascinating looking at the covers through Steve's eye for the strange and bizarre, especially those I was familiar with but had never seen in this context (mind you it was also good to not find anything I'd ever done here, despite Q Magazine once calling one of my covers 'clawfisted'!).

For this book rather than just reprint a load of sleeves, I was keen to try and dig around and find out why the covers ended up the way they did, and the stories behind them. I've worked to record label deadlines, once given just two hours to turn round an LP sleeve for an indie label (happily it was for a punk poet and comedian, and I had access to their xerox machine!), so have sympathy for problems these cause. And sometimes musicians have very determined ideas and cannot be swayed. I recall one release for

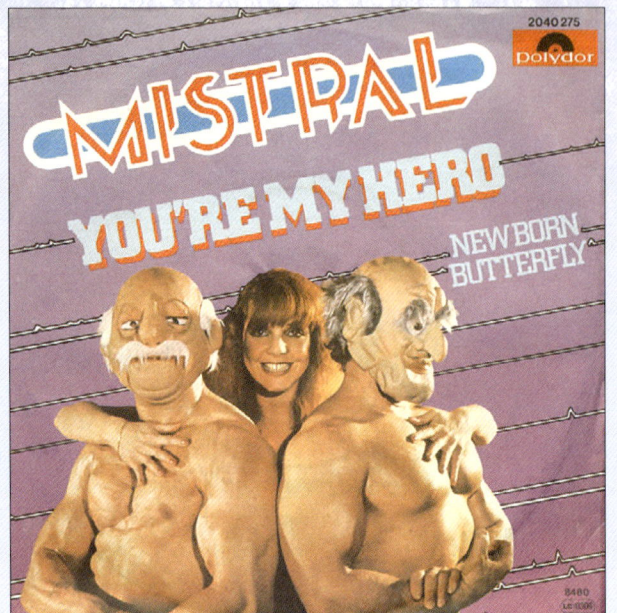

a female singer who had chosen the cover shot and that was that. As my RPM partner's verdict was that she *"was the vainest person I have ever met"* we decided any attempt to change things would be fruitless. And don't get me started on David Coverdale complaining about the colour of wine in the glass on the front of one Deep Purple reissue.

Where curiosity got the better of me I corresponded with some of the people involved, and we also document cases of the artists themselves rubbishing their own covers.

Often the background stories to some of the covers have proved every bit as mad (or in a couple of cases, disturbing) as the images.

Steve puts his exhibition on under The Worst Record Covers In The World banner which is great at drawing people along, but seemed too pejorative for the book title so we've gone with the term 'bizarre'; after all, few people set out to make their sleeve the worst! Plus there are endless 'worst sleeve' galleries on the web, most recycling increasingly grotty jpegs from older listings in an attempt to get traffic. Even the Daily Mail has had a go. Out of interest I tracked one such image and found the exact same poor image file on 37 different sites before tracking the owner in Brazil and getting hold of the original. There have even been a couple of cheapo books too, but hopefully we have done this fascinating genre of album covers justice.

So most of the sleeves are taken off Steve's LPs *. scanned 120% life size to reproduce better. Covers using strange card or textures we photographed rather than scanned to avoid glare. Retouching was kept to a minimum, usually the wear and tear on a record adds to the story. Some of these LPs are now astonishingly rare and fetch three figures if they can be found, so in a few cases we have had to get images from other sources.

There are no CDs. This doesn't mean there are no bizarre CD covers, just that vinyl displays so much better and goes back a lot further. There is a reason the range of vinyl on sale now dwarfs the CD racks at HMV.

Steve of course is still collecting and it's fun trying to hit him with suggestions for sleeves to chase down; it's rare to find one he isn't already aware of but very satisfying when we do! If you can help, reach him through links at the end of this book. And keep an eye out for an exhibition near you.

Simon Robinson

* well only one or two aren't, out of sheer desperation, indicated in the text!
Details of the sleeves shown in the book introduction pages are given on page 178

# HERE PUSSY

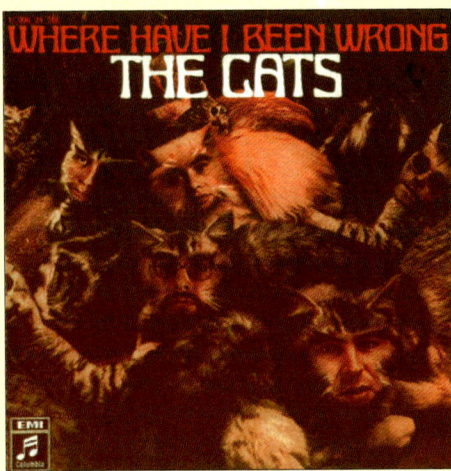

**The Cats • 45 Lives**
Rare Earth / USA / 1970
*Art direction Curtis McNair. Design concept / graphic supervision Tom Schlesinger. Photographer Bart Harris. Artwork by Album Graphics, Inc.*

If you had to chose the top five strangest sleeves in this book, 45 Lives would have to be in there, uncannily like a still from the brilliantly awful *Cats* film of recent years. This Sixties Dutch rock group were largely unknown outside the country, despite a sojourn in America in the mid-1970s and a big (and rather good) German hit *One Way Wind*. The American label Rare Earth (founded by Motown as a way of moving into the rock and underground scene, and named after the band) picked up on The Cats' subtle orchestrated soft rock and tried out this compilation in 1970, their only release on the label. The cover was put together by Motown's in house crew of McNair and Schlesinger but Bart Harris may have done the montage, using the faces off a photo by Harry Pot (right) supplied by the Dutch label. Harris did a lot of sleeve portraits in 1970 (before moving on to other creative fields), but none were as strange or creepy as this. The image was also used on a German 7" sleeve. *Sam Deen and bassist Arnold Muhren helped us piece together the story.*

**El Gato • Gato Barbieri**
RCA / UK / 1975
*Photographers Chuck Stewart, David Hecht, Dwayne Dalrymple. Art directors Acy Lehman, Dick Smith.*

Perhaps even more frightening than The Cats is this one simply called The Cat. It's actually Argentinian saxophonist and composer Leondro 'El Gato' (The Cat) Barbieri, montaged together with a cat photo to produce an image which would not look out of place on a Hammer Horror film poster, but must have put many a prospective buyer off the album. The cat-less image is used on the reverse but by then it's too late and prospective buyers will have run off screaming. Despite his nickname, it was the only time Barbieri used a cat on any of his sleeves, so he must have learned his lesson.

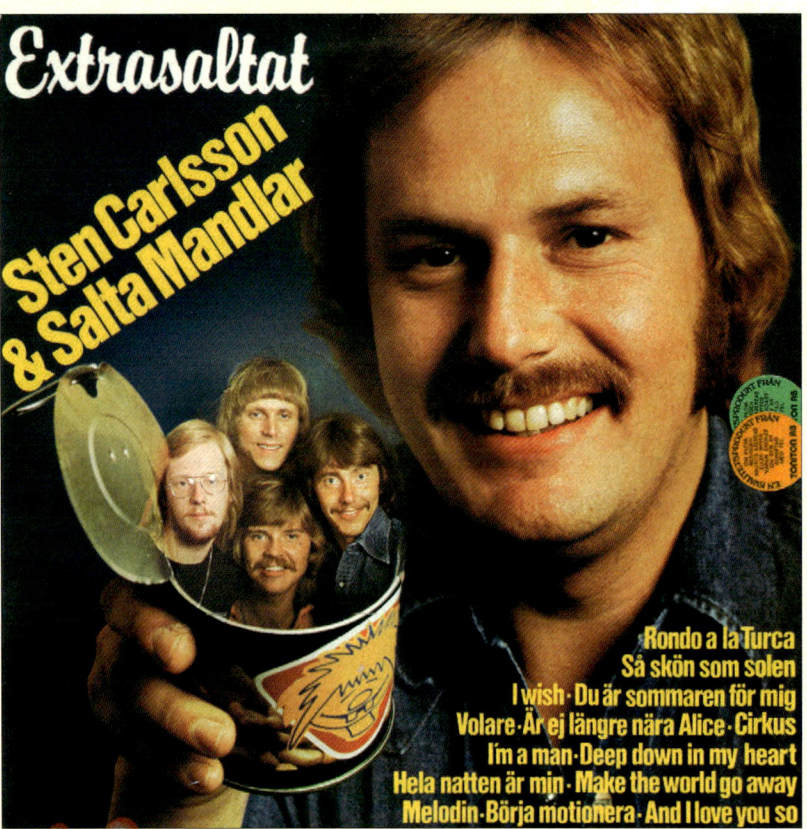

## YOU ARE WHAT YOU EAT

**Gerhard Polt • Leberkäs Hawaii**
Jupiter Records / Germany / 1981

Who says the Germans lack a sense of humour? According to the interweb, Leberkäs is a liver pate with bits of cheese in it, while Polt himself is a Bavarian comedian, satarist and more. Which still doesn't explain this strange sleeve. It's the ketchup which adds the final grim touch to the dish! If you are better at languages than me it's now available as part of a 9CD set off his website.

**Dave McKenna and The Wilbur Little Quartet • Oil & Vinegar**
Honeydew Records / USA / 1977 *[page 4]*
*Cover, design, photography Bob Muller*

They did things differently in the Seventies it's true, but even so! This mind boggling cover was the brainchild of Bob Muller at Idea Plant Inc. who did a lot of, covers for the short lived Honeydew Records, but nothing he or the label did looked anything like as strange as this. McKenna later dismissed the album as sounding like it was recorded in a toilet ... *"and I never got paid."* Noted backing singer Sharon Redd is the woman on the cover, who later had a short but successful solo career. And the Dymo brail? This copy spent most of it's life in a public library.

**Sten Carlson & Salta Mandlar • Extrasaltat**
T Bone Records / Sweden / 1977
*Layout Åke Jacobsson, Photography By Sven Jönsson*

Music archivists suggest this Swedish group encompass (deep breath) soul, pop, schlager, funk *and* classic rock. Not that you'd pick up on any of that from the sleeve photo. Though we are left in no doubt who the leader of the band was, with his band, Salted Almonds, relegated to the tin or, on this previous album (left) a matching set of pink flared touser and shirts. After calling LP *Extra Salty* they kind of ran out of puns on the band's name, posed for a sensible cover portrait on their follow up and then called it a day. And those little stickers at the edge of the album? They proved the album had not been opened and played before you bought it. And yes, salted nuts did come packaged in small tins back then to solve the problem of keeping them fresh before plastic foil was invented.

**Lothar and the Hand People • Presenting**
Capitol / USA / 1968

Lothar only issued two albums, this was the first, reissued minus a few songs a couple of years later. New to us, allow Rolling Stone magazine to elaborate: *"electronic country, a kind of good-time music played by mad dwarfs, and it is really good to listen to."*
They told us what they could recall about the cover. At the suggestion of producer Bob Margouleff, the band shots were taken by an old-school photographer in downtown New York City whose speciality was hand tinting photos (and old school skill). No one recalls his name. It looks like they were mimicking those old high school yearbook images beloved of 'what they looked like then' compilers. Apparently these were to be part of a sleeve concept which proved *"too outrageous"* for Capitol Records (though sadly nobody can recall what it was!). The label's art department then took over and used the photos on the front. The end result is really quite disturbing! And Lothar? The name of their portable synthesiser.

**Bryan Smith • Goes To Town (with His Happy Piano)**  Dansan / UK / 1983

Dansan Records specialised in music for ballroom dancing and Bryan Smith was a stalwart of the label throughout the Seventies and Eighties (indeed he kicked their catalogue off). But if they knew their market, Dansan's grasp of cover design (many by Dan Galvin) was often sadly lacking. CONT...

BRIAN SMITH CONT... For *In Your Own Backyard* they simply got Bryan to pose in his garage, then set the flash gun to stun. *Goes To Town?* Pose him in his sheepskin jacket across from the houses of parliament and reply on daylight to save the cost of a flash-bulb.

As this generation of ballroom dancers pass on, these records now fill the boxes in charity shops, though many are being hawked about on CD and even Apple Music by President Records, who now own the rights. Who needs Strictly?

**Willie Brady • An Irish Evening With**
Avoca Records / Ireland - USA / 1962

Irish ballad and country singer Brady issued no fewer than four albums of Irish Freedom Songs and similar fare in the late Fifties and early Sixties mostly for the Irish / American label Avoca, usually with his head cut-out in a shamrock shape or similar Irish folk cliché. On this occasion the label coughed up for a rare full colour cover but did poor old Brady no favours with this very stagey and awkward looking portrait, possibly after an afternoon down the pub. Mind you social historians will enjoy the interior details; the peat fire, Staffordshire pottery figures, decorative wallpaper borders and Gran in her favourite chair. Sadly Brady, whose musical output rather than his album covers is well regarded today, died very young after a kidney transplant failure in 1969.

# F F F F FASHION

**Die Tanzrhytmiker Und Der Robert Pappert-Chor •
Heute Geht's Rund** Perl Serie / Germany / 1969

"Today it's all about"… is the title; well if only we knew. Pappert was a choir master but here seems to be slumming it on one of the Metronome budget label's cheesy but fascinating German "schlager" collections. But then you start to wonder about the striped Victorian swimwear (which also appeared en masse on an earlier album of the same title - below - from Telefunken), and, following that, the very strange dress hand painted with a grotesque face. Before noticing that the gentleman next to her has his zip undone. Die Super-Stimmungsbombe indeed.

**The Royal Wedding • H.R.H. The Prince Andrew &
Miss Sarah Ferguson**
BBC Records / UK / 1986

While this album may have seemed run of the mill at the time, over thirty five years later (and twenty five years after they divorced) we look at it with very different feelings. The BBC issued numerous souvenir albums of the royal weddings they broadcast, in showy gatefold sleeves. Judging by the way they turn up in mint condition in charity shops, they didn't get played too often.

# JODELFEEST

**De Alpen Zusjes • Als Er Wat Te Feesten Valt**
Telstar / Netherlands / 1989 7" single

The cover here almost demands a speech balloon competition! Eproctofilie *is* a thing, and if you want to look it up then just don't tell us. Otherwise, Dutch duo The Alpine Sisters are living proof of the adage *'if at first you don't succeed'*, issuing their first single in 1981 but having to wait thirty years for their first big hit. And they still look remarkably ageless today, though this turns out to be thanks to a rotating line up rather than the rejuvenating powers of Combray face cream. The original Alpine Sisters, and only one of them (Carla Janssen-Langendijk, the blonde on the sleeve) stayed the course, packed it in around 2009. A new couple then took over the name (with permission), had that big hit, and became a party vocal brand, swopping members as and when to this day. Most of the early single sleeves played on their ever tightening shorts which seem to have been their visual trademark. They even teamed up for a single with our old friend Cock Van Der Palm, with the word COCK in capital letters in case you missed the inference. Check out their web site and book them!

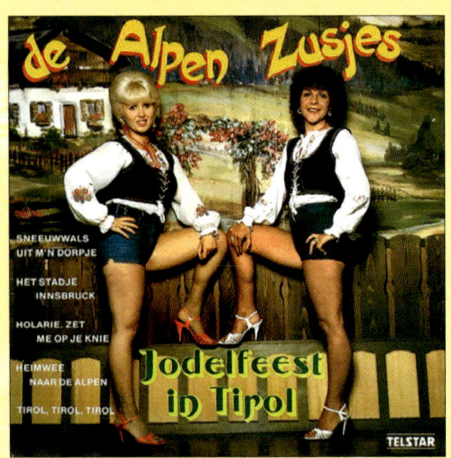

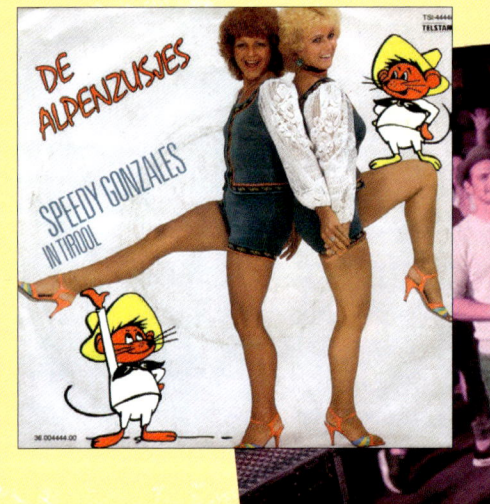

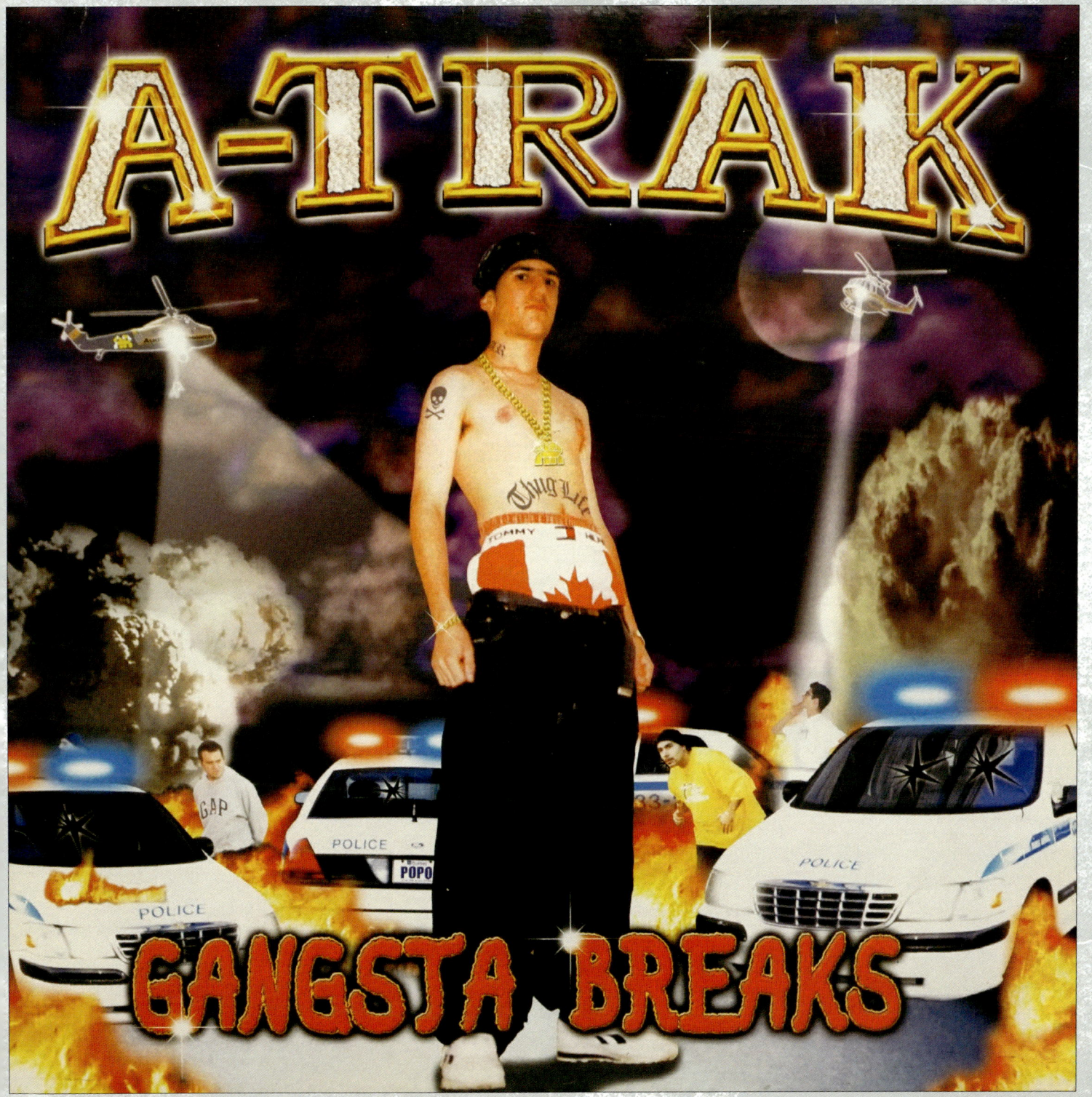

# Gangsta Briefs

### Trick Daddy • www.thug.com
Slip N Slide Records - Atlantic / USA / 1998
*Graphic Design Society Productions, Inc.*

You are now "on-line"! Indeed. This cover reaches a level of awfulness even in an area of music not noted for a sense of design or taste. Trick (Maurice Young) came from one of the grimmest of childhood backgrounds turning to music as a way out of crime after being released from prison, so there are positives here, although he clearly didn't take design classes while inside. A curious mess of out of date browser imagery and a low-res jpeg portrait. It's not as if it was a low-budget production; double vinyl, colour sleeve, inner bag and all the trimmings. Happily Maurice's more recent albums have seen things improve a lot. Time to go back and rework this?

### A-Trak • Gangsta Breaks
Arnmo Records / USA / 2001 12" single
*Art direction, design and layout P-Thugg*

Real or self parody? Either way it's dreadful! Bad boy A-Trak (real name Alain Macklovitch), Canadian DJ, turntableist, producer and record label exec., has all the gangsta cliches here, clip art for the broken windscreens, trousers round ankles, trainers and bling. The record is nothing more than a series of unexciting drum loops. Monkeyboy (left) is just creepy. AT found fame in the duo Duck Sauce, with a 2010 worldwide hit *Barbra Streisand*. Quack!

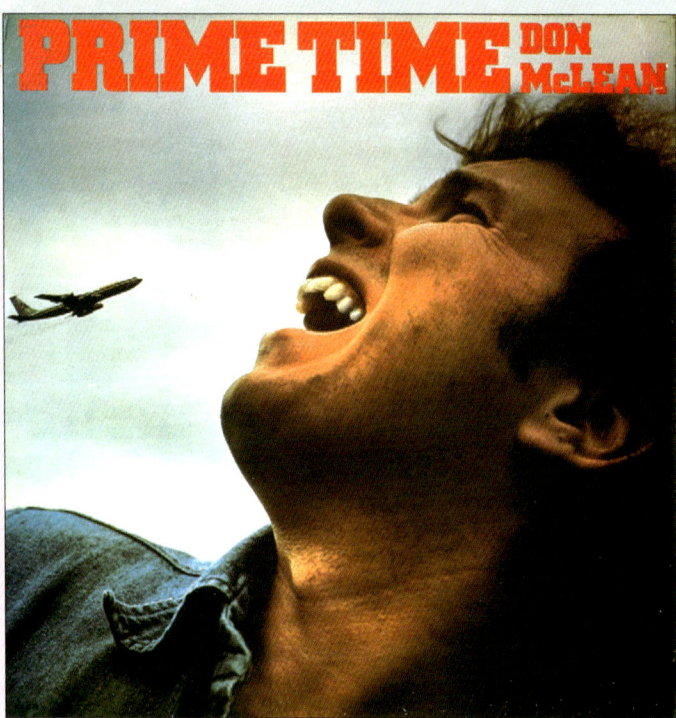

### Don McLean • Prime Time
EMI / UK / 1977
*Photography and design Herb Gart. Steve Saltman of Chrome Print - Cibachrome. Art direction Howard Fritzson*

Well *somebody* must have liked the idea of McLean looking like he was about to have an aircraft fly up his nose. It's all a bit like those comedy holiday snaps where you pose trying to push the tower of Pisa upright. Apart from the excellent *American Pie* sleeve, Don generally did moody don't-rock-the-boat cover shots, so we have

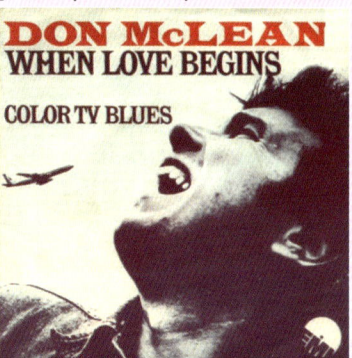

no idea if it was meant as a joke or just an idea that went a bit askew (it also appeared on this Dutch 45 but looks no better in monochrome). Although it is noticeable that when this album was finally licensed for CD twenty years later it appeared in a more neutral sleeve designs in Europe and America too.

# PAINT BY NUMBERS

**V/A • Fiddle Me Jig**
MFP / UK / 1978

Being on EMI's budget label Music For Pleasure may explain the cover's inept watercolour. Painted montages were a mainstay of the label's compilations but were often quite skilled pieces (they even used noted film poster artist Tom Chantrell a couple of times). This one looks like an 'O' Level art entry. We have heads emerging from green ooze, violin bows sticking through necks, and the main character wearing a gum shield.

**Scottish Sing-a-Long**
London / UK / 1960

This on the other hand is a skilled but quite terrifying piece of work. The anonymous image of a hirsute sergeant major in mid-bellow is hardly one to show your kids. Arranged by conductor Ivor Raymonde (Simon from The Cocteau Twins' dad) the album only appeared in the UK and Canada. The Australians later picked it up for the Ace Of Clubs budget label and wisely replaced the cover with a photograph of a Scottish park!

**Bobby Bland • The Best Of Vol 2**
Duke Records / USA / 1968
*Design Richard Simpson*

The Bobby Bland cover above left is the work of jazz and gospel producer Richard Simpson, who also wrote the sleeve notes and co-ordinated the track list for Duke Records. He has obviously been influenced by David Stone Martin's noted jazz sleeves but missed the mark by some margin. Was there a Volume 1? Indeed (left), also by Simpson and slightly better in that you can actually recognise the musician. Bobby didn't have much luck with his covers, the terrible broken heart image (far left) was also on the Duke label.

19

# Paint By Numbers

**Scotch • Evolution**
Beat Box / Sweden / 1984
*Illustration Adriano Merigo*

The Euro debut album from an Eighties' Italian disco outfit who had scored with *Disco Band* in the charts (if No. 4 in Switzerland counts as a hit!). The album came out in dozens of countries, all of which went with this warped airbrush image of a guy in his tinsel trunks marching over the landscape holding a concrete ghetto blaster for the cover, being followed by a line of vaguely dinosaur looking critters; nobody seems to know why. And Chris Foss the artist clearly wasn't. Nor did anybody question the cover, except in South Africa, where is was dropped in favour of this just as bad streetwise cartoon style illustration.

**The Hollies • Five Three One - Double Seven O Four**
Polydor / UK / 1979
*illustrator Jack Wood*

The Hollies transformed from a polished Sixties harmony pop group into a polished AOR harmony soft rock album band in the Seventies. The sleeve sort of mirrors the struggle. Guitarist Terry Sylvester is credited with the idea, which is kind of a nice party trick (especially if you recall playing visual games like this on your calculator) but even with noted sleeve illustrator Jack Wood at the drawing board (he had done covers for Status Quo, Thin Lizzy and The Sensational Alex Harvey Band) it just looks very bland. Nothing dates like technology.

**Jon Lord • Gemini Suite**
Purple Records / UK / 1971
*Jim Willis, Westfore Design cover*

This strange homerotic illustration runs across front and back of this gatefold referencing the titular sign of the zodiac, but while the illustration works in places, the faces would throw recognition technology. America gave it the thumbs down and replaced it right away, and even a recent vinyl reissue went with new art, though arguably not much better. Jon Lord was a founding member of Deep Purple, here on his second classical / rock hybrid outing.

# SAY CHEESE

### Glen Daly • A Hundred Thousand Welcomes
Golden Guinea Pye / UK / 1972

Posing outside the "famous" Ashfield Social Club in Glasgow (which is where it was taped and is frankly as unprepossessing building as you are ever likely to see on an album sleeve), one just wonders why they chose the only shot on the roll where Daly (christened Bartholomew Francis McGovern McCann Dick) has his eyes firmly shut. He was headlining the venue's first Summer Show, a three month season in which Daly and others played weekly with special guests stopping by.

Pye's budget label Golden Guinea offered distribution to less well known musicians who nevertheless might have a niche market, and this was Daly's fourth album for them (he received a silver disc for Scottish sales presented by the Lord Provost of Glasgow). It was also released in Canda and New Zealand, reason (and chart placings) unknown.

The Ashfield (see left, 404 Hawthorn Street) is still standing - just - but appears to have been closed for some years ("*the worst function venue I have attended in fifty years,*" being one of the last reviews before the shutters came down) and now looks very different to the neat and tidy frontage of fifty years ago.

### Vašo Patejdl • Lov Na City
Opus Records / Czechoslovakia / 1987
*Photo A Molnar. Design M Brocko*

We'd all probably look a bit daft if photographed drinking through a straw, so the idea is surely to avoid it? Otherwise it might end up looking like a dental suction tool... It's an astonishingly dull cover, all the stranger given Vašo's previous solo album debut (he'd been part of the noted Czech pop rock band Elan) had been a well executed full-on Hipgnosis style affair. We like the glass too, which reminds us of those seaside novelty ones where all the clothes fall off when it is filled.

### Dean Reed • A Jeho Svet
Supraphon / Czechoslovakia / 1977
*Cover Pavel Jasansky*

I have this idea of myself as a huge tree, with all branches for hair and the trunk as my neck, do you think that would work for the cover? Well sadly the answer is no, but they went ahead and tried it anyway. But only in Czechoslovakia. Bulgaria and the GDR went with much more sensible covers. Reed was actually American but moved to Europe and then settled in East Germany where he had a lot of success. Just not with sleeves.

# F F FASHION

**Orion • Reborn**
Sun Records / USA / 1979
*Cover Betty M. Cherry*

Whoever stitched this blue satin ensemble together needs to adjust the tension on their sewing machine. It is resolutely low-rent show-biz style at its best (or worst). Digging in to Orion's story there is a Kendo Nagasaki theme here, as he posed in a mask for ALL his album covers. Signed to Sun Records and with more than a passing vocal similarity to Elvis Presley, the label played on this unashamedly after Presley's death. Orion (real name James Hughes Bell) also wore the mask and often Elvis style jump suits on stage until the early Eighties.

Indeed the earlier pressing of this album had an astonishingly tasteless cover of Elvis lying in an open coffin and Orion walking over him (above) which was quickly replaced. It's a story which has since inspired a remarkable film documentary (look on iPlayer) but the story does not end well, so be prepared.

**Dolly Parton • Bubbling Over**
RCA Victor / USA / 1973

This surreal effort bucked the trend of Dolly's sleeves, which generally focussed on the woman herself in carefully staged studio shoots. It was taken by Nashville photographer Les Leverett (official photographer for The Grand Ole Opry in Nashville from 1960-1992) who recalled that originally RCA wanted a shot of Dolly in a one-piece leaping up à la The Beatles' *Twist And Shout*. Having tried this, Les and his wife decided the results were far too revealing! His wife suggested the fountain at the Country Music Hall of Fame for a reshoot. Who thought of floating Dolly's disembodied head in the fountain we don't know.

And yet it won Billboard's Best Country Cover of the year 1973. In her book *Dolly Parton, Songteller: My Life in Lyrics* she commented on the image: "We tried to use the fountain. It's an awful picture of me. We kept working and working on that picture, trying to make it look right. We needed that fountain and we kept trying to superimpose my face on it. It's just one of those mistakes you make."

> **DOLLY PARTON—Bubbling Over.** RCA 1-0286. Dolly must write a dozen or so hits a week, and since Porter Wagoner resumed his writing career, he's almost keeping pace. The two of them supply the bulk of the material for this, another in the huge collection of Dolly's album outputs, and it—as the others before it—tops the last one out. It ranges from the happy up-tempo to the tearful ballad, and no one fills this range better than Dolly.
> Best cuts: "Love With Me," "Pleasant As May," "Love, You're So Beautiful Tonight."
> Dealers: Excellent photographic work on the cover, by the old master Les Leverett.

## Rudolf Víg • Magyarországi Cigány Népdalok (Gypsy Folk Songs From Hungary)
Hungaroton / Hungary / 1976
*Sándor Sajnovits design. Roger Beeckmans photography.*

Several Eastern Bloc countries ran their own official state record labels during the Cold War era when much decadent Western music was frowned upon. Hungaroton was one, based in Hungary from 1951 (originally as Qualiton). A feature of such labels was traditional folk and classical music, but while they usually went for travel brochure images of the country, here the label designer has chosen a less flattering image of a happy performer with dental issues and a moustache that could garner prizes at The World Beard & Moustache Championships. And then repeated the shot in flower shapes across the front. It ends up like a twisted still from an early Polanski film, drawing you in if you stare at it too long. I can only imagine the designer was having an off day, as his other work for the label is often excellent. Indeed the rest of this elaborate gatefold cover is pretty groovy. So if Hungarian folk is your thing, you can always turn the sleeve around. Once communism began to fade in the 1980s the label was privatised and continues to thrive.
Music wise the LP includes such patriotic gems as *My Hat Is Covered With Brick Dust*, *I Have Neither Table Nor Chair*, *My Dog's Leg Hurts* and *My Little Worn Cart*.
The Ramones issued their debut album the same year.

## René Et Nathalie • Sur La Plage
GC / Canada / 1983
*Illustration Marcel Goudreau*

There is far too much detail in those teeth for comfort. Many will be familiar with those promenade caricatures where they draw a big nose on a pencil sketch and relieve you of your holiday money, clearly the inspiration here. It was the album's producer who came up with the concept, commissioned it and issued it on his own label.
The French Canadian duo (the Donny and Marie of Quebec) thus portrayed are brother and sister, both of who had successful careers on disc and TV during the 1970s and 1980s and are well known in their home country. They seem to have sung only in French so the market outside Canada (and France) was limited, though as a child star Nathalie was also signed to CBS Sony in Japan.
The cover does makes you smile which I assume was the intention. The smile quickly vanishes when you learn Nathalie was being abused by her manager throughout the Eighties…

# WATERCOLOUR CHALLENGE

**Lasse Dahlquist • Svenska Sångfavoriter**
HMV / Sweden / 1960
*Heruiausson*

Looking like some grotesque 1940s advert for Players Navy Shag, this illustration certainly startles but it also hard not to keep looking at it. So job at least half done. Then you turn it over and see adverts for another half dozen albums in the Svenska Sångfavoriter series, all featuring similarly hefty caricatures. Clearly old Lasse was much loved in Sweden, many of these recordings date from the 1940s and it has been reissued on vinyl a few times and later released on CD. It also features his smash hit of 1941 *Oh, What A Big, Big Boy*.

The cover is the work of Swedish artist Erik Hermansson, who was well known for his illustrations and line drawings in local newspapers and books. He did several record sleeves along similar lines as we can see, some more exaggerated than others (he was much kinder on the female singers). The similarity of Sigge Fürst to Britain's much loved (© BBC website) OAP railcard holder Michael Portillo is very disturbing, while the Povel Ramel cover is just awful. I trust his partner did a Clementine Churchill on it.

Happily most of Hermansson's other work is more restrained, and at times his black and white ink drawings are not unlike those of Robert Crumb. A book of his commercial illustrations was published in Sweden some years ago.

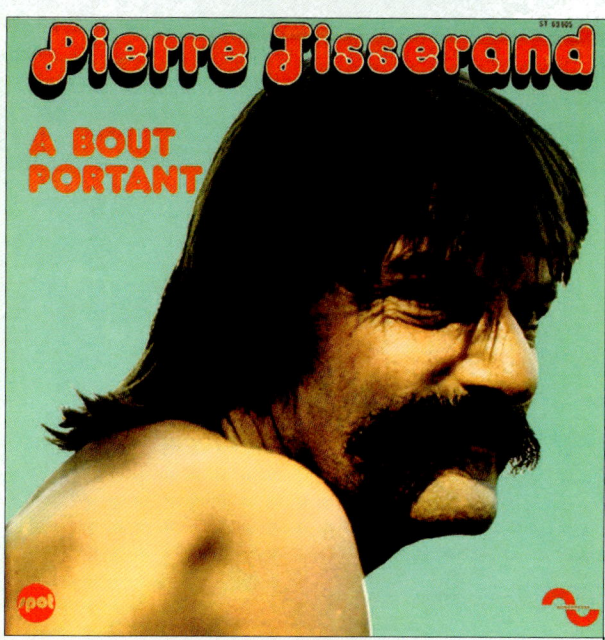

### Pierre Tisserand • Pierre Tisserand
RCA / France / 1978
*Direction artistique Bob Socquet, C. Pavy, G Salmon. P. Tisserand. Illustration pochette Gaston Tisserand.*

Another caricature, which raises so many questions about this noted French singer and writer. First of which has to be; could he not put his trousers on before the artist reached for his pencils? The strange little straw-filled toy boat on wheels also causes scratched heads, the paper boat on the pond is becalmed but the billowing sail suggests storm force ten, while the tiny patch of tilled soil feels like somebody shirks their gardening duties (as does the snail on the spade handle!).
If you're wondering whether the moustache is exaggerated, forget it. Clean shaven on his debut in 1969, the difficult follow-up LP took four years, and one suspects much of that was down to growing this monster. If anything, Pierre's defining facial feature is underplayed, see the photo above! It stayed with him through the Seventies until he stopped recording in 1982. There was a comeback CD in 2003 but by then the moustache had left due to musical differences.

### Marco Bakker • Dunkelrote Rosen
EMI / Holland / 1969

You'd certainly take a step back if Dutch baritone Marco Bakker suddenly loomed out of the rose garden looking like this! Maybe it was a toss up between a record cover or a toothpaste commercial when he went in to the photo studio that morning. Not for the first time in this book we wonder why on earth they chose it, as he looks quite brooding and handsome on the back sleeve. To be fair it was his first album, and he settled into a leather recliner on the follow up (and smart casual for trips to Italy, below). Marco is still performing, and giving vocal masterclasses well into his 80s.

MOONRIDE
ANATOMY
BRAIN ROT
WATCHING THE TIME GO BY
NOTHING LEFT TO GIVE

(Kopperdisc Records - Nov., 1974)
9014NB

TRUCKIN' ON
TALES UNTOLD
MAGIC IN YOUR MIND
A THOUSAND WARRIORS
WISE MAN
DREAMS

### Kopperfield • Tales Untold
Kopperdisc / USA / 1974

No band name on the cover or spine, no catalogue number or production credits - we are in private pressing land again. All the details were hidden on a fold-out lyric sheet inside.

They clearly had very little grasp of pen and ink technique either, the front cover would probably challenge Battleaxe's claim to worst metal art ever (next page!), had anybody outside Michigan ever heard of them. Kopperfield seem to have spent more time designing their own boy-band style logo for the back cover than worrying about how cheap their watery tribute to Conan The Barbarian looks. We particularly like the way the album title is hand drawn on two pieces of paper then pasted in place; I know rub-down lettering wasn't cheap but Blick did a more than passable 'olde english' sheet. It's a good job the axe man is left handed too, he looks like he'd struggle to knock the skin off a rice pudding with his other arm, although the three headed snake doesn't look like it would put up that much of a contest. And it might be worth getting in a structural surveyor to give that tower foundation on the side a quick once over.

Kopperfield, formed in 1971 from two rival school bands, toured a lot in the area, later opening for bigger out of town bands, and released this album to sell at shows and garner interest in a major record deal, before calling it a day a year later. The band were voted into the Michigan Rock and Roll Legends Hall of Fame in 2020. Like a lot of obscure Seventies' rock LPs it has since generated any number of reissues and CD bonus tracks to satisfy collectors.

And dig that amazing Kopperdisc Records logo on the back too.

### Twisted Sister • Stay Hungry
Atlantic / USA / 1984

*Art Direction Bob Defrin. T.s. Bone Logo Conceived And Designed By Dee Snider. Costume And Makeup Design Suzette Guilot-Snider. Photography By Mark Weiss Studios*

More heavy glam-metal (Dee Snider considers the term to be inappropriate) tomfoolery (*Stay Hungry* is not a cover of the Talking Heads first album gem). The sleeve image looks exactly like what it was, some pillock with a cow-bone trying to come across all frightening in a photo studio, but ending up looking like a prat. The back is even funnier, as Dee is carrying on in a similar fashion while the rest of the band (ALL of them in the de riguer sleeveless denim tops) just calmly sit next to him. It's as if they were on a weekly visit to their idiot brother in an asylum. Still, this was the album which saw them go mainstream, three million people bought it (and our copy looks like it was blu-taced to someone's bedroom wall at one stage!). The awful TS logo outlasted the band (they spilt three years after this LP), and morphed into a trademark which appears on reissues, merchandise and live albums to this day.

# LEATHERS

**Battleaxe • Burn This Town**
Music For Nations / UK / 1983
*Illustration Arthur Ball*

Here's another illustration which struggles to make the grade. We are not the only people to think the choice of Arthur's only sleeve painting was ill-advised as it has now been repackaged three times.
Talking to North East cultural historian Gary Alikivi in 2014, singer Dave King explained how the initial sleeve came about. "The record company boss asked us what we wanted on the album cover. We had a friend and local artist called Arthur Ball who came up with a basic idea of a biker on his motorbike wielding an axe, with a town in the background burning down, it looked like Sunderland! We sent that off in the mail to head office at Roadrunner in Holland.
We waited weeks and really needed to know from the boss what his thoughts were on the idea. Two months later the album was released, we couldn't believe they had gone and used the draft cover idea as the finished art work."
Since then the cover is regularly rated one of the worst heavy metal album covers ever, despite some stiff competition. The French demanded a new cover when they put it out a year later (below left) and it was re-released here with a more finished version (top left) of the original concept, relocated to London (and with a second logo), although there remain some questionable aspects to the biker's proportions! As the CD age came round the band also sported a new (and it has to be said horrible) third logo which replaced the painting altogether. Finally, come the 30th anniversary, Steamhammer went to town with bonus tracks, remastering AND a fourth new cover (left). This time Louise Limb was asked to re-imagine the original concept and did a pretty good job too, though to date it has not made it to vinyl (come on, if Taylor Swift can manage it...).
And in these more enlightened times the biker has also changed sex.

### V/A • Metal Killers
Kastle Killers / UK / 1984
*Art direction / design Shoot That Tiger. Cover Barry Thorpe*

You'd struggle to find *anything* positive to say about this one. The New Wave of British Heavy Metal sprang up largely around a much younger market, and numerous metal labels were quick to issue budget collections at pocket money prices (I remember buying albums like *Age Of Atlantic* when I was a teenager for the same reason, lack of money!). These collections sometimes gave budding fantasy artists a chance to show off, though here you wish they hadn't.

How on earth did our steroid raddled warrior even get his fingers on the frets of that mis-shapen Flying V? And, as far as we know, the Zulus never fought with swords (or had Pterodactyls wheeling above their heads for that matter). Shoot The Tiger (an agency that did lots of good covers) then stole 'killer' off the Iron Maiden LP of the same name, added some neat airbrushing to the title, but forgot to mask out the middle of the A in their rush to get it off the desk. The illustrator was capable of much better, too as his covers for Elvis collections and some classical LPs prove, so perhaps he too was in a hurry. Kastle Killers (part of Castle Communications) tried a Volume 2, with a woman photographed in a leather bikini (causing one dealer I saw to list it as 'heavy cheesecake'!) holding a large axe. A third metal compilation followed before they lost enthusiasm and shut the imprint down.

### Ted Nugent • Scream Dream
Epic / UK / 1980
*Cover photograph Lynn Goldsmith. Bob Heimall, Stephanie Zuras Art direction / design*

Not being a Ted fan, I hadn't really paid much attention to this until Steve put it into his exhibition. But he's right, it is ludicrous. The Nuge meets The Terminator, only our Ted turns his arms into guitars rather than nasty stabbing spikes. There is no real point to it whatsoever, all overwrought *"once more with feeling Ted"* screaming into Lynn's lens (much like the music really), while the post-studio montage work is inept even for pre-Photoshop days. The inner sleeve (below leftß) is more down to earth suggesting something beyond raw meat-eating Ted existed, but marketing wise that would have been a no no. Mind you even there he cannot resist holding a gun in case we doubt his masculinity.

# ... AND SPANDEX STUDS

**Rabbit • Too Much Rock'n'Roll**
CBS / Australia / 1976
*Design J. Peter Thoeming / Photography Carroll Holloway*

What a difference a year makes. Rabbit favoured the down to earth rock 'n roll look on the back of their first album (right) in 1975. Then someone got them a copy of Creem's Glam Rock special and it all went downhill fashion wise. As with Raven (below), you wonder who thought this would be a good look. *"The pinnacle of Australian glam rock"* (according to an Australian rock historian) the cover includes all the metal cliches; a mostly impossible to read logo, ill-fitting spandex, charity shop accessories and boots which (along with the fire-eating on stage) were a guarantee of frequent trips to A&E. Plus the guy on the right looks like he just photobombed the session. Nor does coming from Australia excuse it, and though this almost made the Top 50 there they split in 1977. The condition of the sleeve suggests this copy has enjoyed a party life-style almost as much as the group themselves!

**Raven • The Pack Is Back**
Atlantic / USA / 1986
*Art Direction Bob Defrin, Design Concept Tony Incigeri, Photography Mark Weiss.*

Whatever the musical merits of the New Wave Of British Heavy Metal, their reliance on often childish cover art set them apart from their Seventies' peers. Raven serve as a prime example across 15 album covers which range from the dull to the absurd, with a logo looking like it was designed by a sixth former with a felt pen and a Helix unbreakable plastic ruler during a rainy lunch break. Formed in 1974, Raven issued their first album in 1981 but signing to Atlantic in 1984 began to tweak their sound and look towards the US market. Hence the sartorial inelegance here where they wore underwear over spandex for the first time. The lockers they are bursting out of have been artfully damaged but fail to convince. The only surprise is they didn't add a shaky camera effect. Producer Incigeri came up with it°, and Weiss (who specialised in Eighties metal sleeves) did his best, but struggled. Rollerball has a lot to answer for!

## DISCO DUCKS

**Eclipse • Night And Day**
Casablanca USA 1978
*Logo design Bob Lemm. Front cover photo Daniel Poulin. Front cover art Michel 'Zappy' Durr. Graphics Gribbitt!*

Like everyone else seeing this, Steve assumed someone's younger brother had done the eyes in tippex and felt pen… An 8 minute disco dance version of The Kinks *You Really Got Me* anyone? You have been warned. Then Steppenwolf's *Born To Be Wild*, rated on at least one prog rock site as *"the worst cover of any kind"*. Until you hit Donovan's *Sunshine Superman*. Nor do we understand this album's confused story of two very different covers. The photograph of the band looks fairly new wave-ish, until we get to the guy on the left, with those pupils painted on his eyelids. Somebody like Sparks might have pulled it off but here it makes for a deeply disturbing look. So much so that in their native Canada and elsewhere it was relegated to the back, as they rightly figured it might put buyers off. They used the overdesigned 'logo' instead (right). Spare a thought for confused hard-core Eclipse fans too; the band's debut had been a much admired Pink Floyd inspired prog rock synth fest. There was no third album.

**Quim Barreiros • Recebi Um Convite (À Casa Da Jóquina) / Roubaram-me A Mocidade E Os Amigos**
Fénix Records / Portugal / 1975 7" single
*Fotografia Nick Boothman*

With over a *hundred* singles and albums behind him in his native Portugal since the early 1970s, if there were an award for 'most sleeve photos badly taken with a flashbulb' Quim would walk away with it.
But for some reason on the single overleaf he decided to be snapped naked in a photo studio, save for his accordion. *"I received an invitation (To the house of Joquina)"* sings Quim (in Portugese), but we never learn if it said 'clothes optional'. Or what Joquina thought about it all. Or indeed what he is doing with the sausage on the cassette (left). Quim is still going strong with a CD *Educacao Sexual* out as recently as 2020… And that name? Short for Joaquim. Probably too late to change it now.

# SOMETHING FOR THE LADIES

**Fab Company • Our Songs For You**
Aspen Records / 1977
*Photography Steve Frink / Cover Concept, Design and Production Media Graphics*

FAB Company (FAB being the first letters of their three christian names, we don't know if they were Thunderbirds' fans) came out of the late Sixties' folk rock boom in Denver with a smart first 1969 album sleeve cover shot, courtesy of Stylist Records. This third LP on small time local label Aspen in Colorado suggests they had expanded to a quartet (but were back as a trio for a final live album two years later). Quite what inspired them to go topless for this one we don't know, but with the strange glowing Readybrek effect and that title we assumed it was another set of true believers at first (either that or they were into the whole sharing a sauna thing). Nothing much else is known about the group, though one of them issued a comedy album a few years later and their catalogue has appeared on download sites in recent years so somebody is still rooting for them.

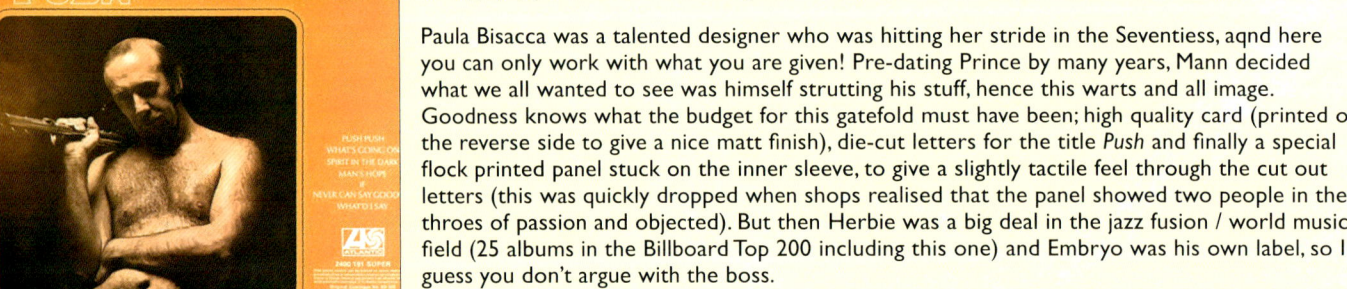

**Herbie Mann • Push Push**
Embryo Cotillion Records / USA / 1971
*Photography Joel Brodski. Album design Paula Bisacca*

Paula Bisacca was a talented designer who was hitting her stride in the Seventiess, aqnd here you can only work with what you are given! Pre-dating Prince by many years, Mann decided what we all wanted to see was himself strutting his stuff, hence this warts and all image. Goodness knows what the budget for this gatefold must have been; high quality card (printed on the reverse side to give a nice matt finish), die-cut letters for the title *Push* and finally a special flock printed panel stuck on the inner sleeve, to give a slightly tactile feel through the cut out letters (this was quickly dropped when shops realised that the panel showed two people in the throes of passion and objected). But then Herbie was a big deal in the jazz fusion / world music field (25 albums in the Billboard Top 200 including this one) and Embryo was his own label, so I guess you don't argue with the boss.

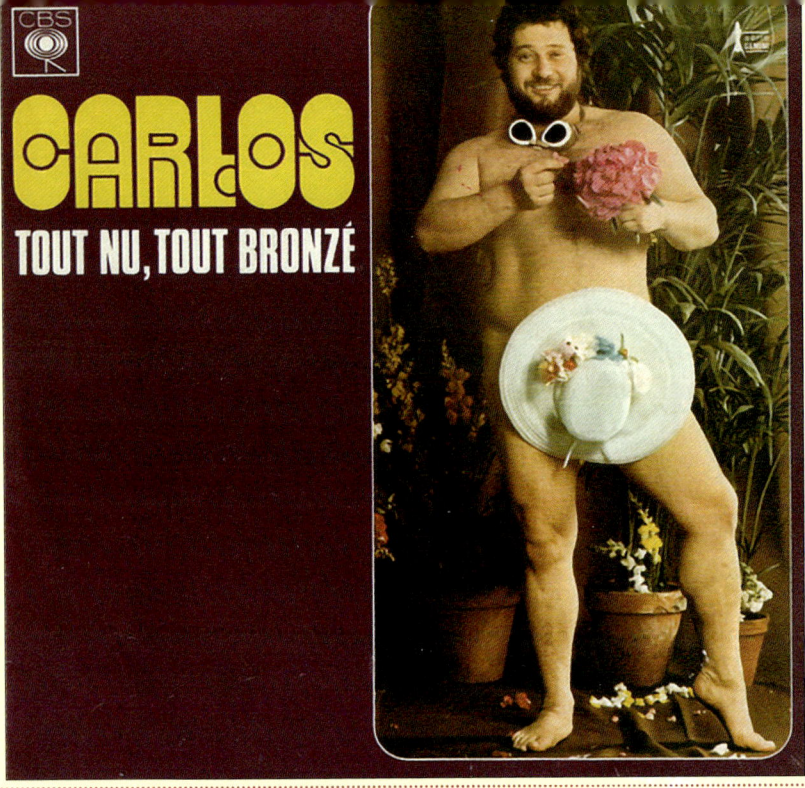

# SOMETHING FOR THE LADIES

### Carlos • Hier... Aujourd'hui
Pathe Marconi EMI / Canada / 1981
*Photo M Jeanneau Télé Star. Direction Artistique Jacques Plait*

Yvan-Chrysostome Dolto, Carlos to his mates, had a dozen albums out in his native France, some also issued in Canada, as here. Most involved terrible punning titles (*Tropi Carlos* being my favourite) and strange covers, though he clearly didn't take it all too seriously. However *Yesterday... Today* (a compilation originally issued in France as *Disque D'Or*) is one which might have benefitted from a 'hang on a minute' moment at Pathé Records, with the eye drawn inexorably towards the porpoise no matter how hard you try and look away. There is quite a lot of photo retouching going on here as well; the exotic ferns are montaged in and some strange airbrushing-out of who knows what has gone on below his name too. Maybe the lucky photographer had caught themself in the bathroom mirror. Nor was it Carlos' first topless sleeve, *Tout Nu, Tout Bronzé* (*All Naked, All Tanned*) (left) features him wearing nothing but a hat.

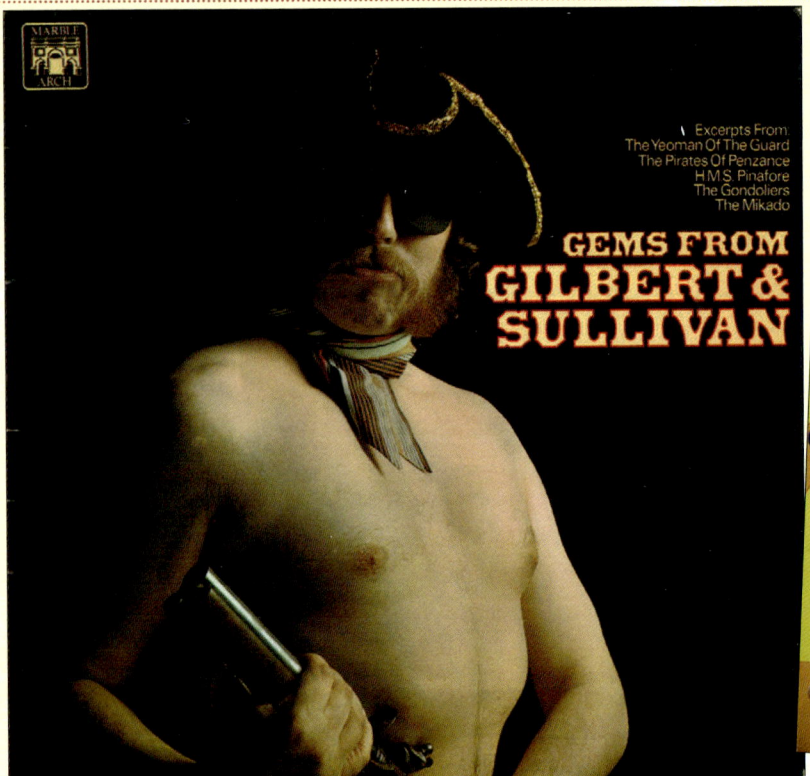

### V/A • Gems From Gilbert & Sullivan
Pye Marble Arch / UK / 1969

Somebody must have thought this would sell a few records! But if so they left their names off the sleeve.
Pye had their own in house design team and in 1969 most of them were more interested in the pop side of things than repackaging old recordings for their budget label Marble Arch (or cheap compilation for Hallmark - see below!). I don't recall reading about any topless performances of *The Pirates of Penzance,* though it was the Sixties so who knows... and it is not unlike some of the mad Westminster Gold classical sleeves later in this book. Steve suggests it has homoerotic overtones; so we look forward to the in-depth Channel 4 'documentary' on the subject.

# SOMETHING FOR THE LADIES

**Alan Franklin • Come Home Baby**
Aladdin Records / USA / 1980
*Album Designed by Peter Colan / Photography Joann Paula Arreola [previous page]*

Who could resist? (Please don't write in.) A glass of chianti, a bundle of dollar bills (that's a $100 on top), a Florida tan and a read of the special double Xmas issue of *High Times* magazine. With goodness knows what to follow. It's a cover that might have just about sneaked through in the Sixties but by 1980 was very dated.

Alan was clearly excited by his first solo album (on which he played everything except drums), so much so that he forgot to put his name on the cover. Or to get dressed. Though he did endearingly remember to dedicate it all to his mum Ethel. On the back he seems to be auditioning to replace Johnny Weismuller in the Tarzan film franchise.

Alan first emerged in the late Sixties with a couple of albums under the name The Alan Franklin Explosion / The Blues Climax (on the Horne label), *"made up of four rebellious wild fanatical musicians who literally go insane on stage,"* according to the cover. Which may explain why such a gap between records. These discs (copyright The Penetration Publishing Co.) are now much sought after garage rarities (one side is a continuous 18 minutes plus of 'unadulterated rock' apparently), though the early sleeve (left) exudes a very home-made quality (the moire pattern is original). The sleeve notes remind his fan base (you could set one up just by writing to Horne Records) that The Blues Climax *"became very popular in Europe."* I can't say I recall them on the UK circuit. Are we sure Alan isn't getting himself confused with The Climax Blues Band?

### Banco • Canto Di Primavera
Ricordi Records / Italy / 1979

In an age when even Nirvana's second album sleeve is being cancelled, it is doubtful whether you would risk this on a 7" single sleeve today. That's singer Francesco Di Giacomo on the front, doing his best Bob Hite impression, holding up his young baby in a swimming pool. Banco were one of the top Italian progressive rock groups of the Seventies but in truth none of their sleeves were especially good (unless you're into shoe juggling, though as Francesco is again starkers on the back we're beginning to see a trend here).

### Bamperos • Tule Kanssani Kylpyyn
Anuco Records / 1980 / Finland

*Kannen layout Mainos Putikki. Kannen kuva Studio Jouko Jarvinen*

This locally successful schlager show band were from Finland, playing clubs and restaurants before going pro in 1973, ditching the old look (below) and going for a 'naked in an iron bath' photo shoot on this, their third LP. Stinginess with the suds (at least we hope it's soap) sadly reveals it to be faked, so the 'most Finnish blokes in a bath' entry for the Guinness Book of Records remains open.
The title track *Come Bath With Me* (we have not made any of this up) is still popular in Finnish karaoke bars, but then it is dark for most of the winter so I guess you have to entertain yourselves somehow. The keyboard player jumped ship to go and dig for gold in Lapland (as you do) but the others soldiered on until 1990.

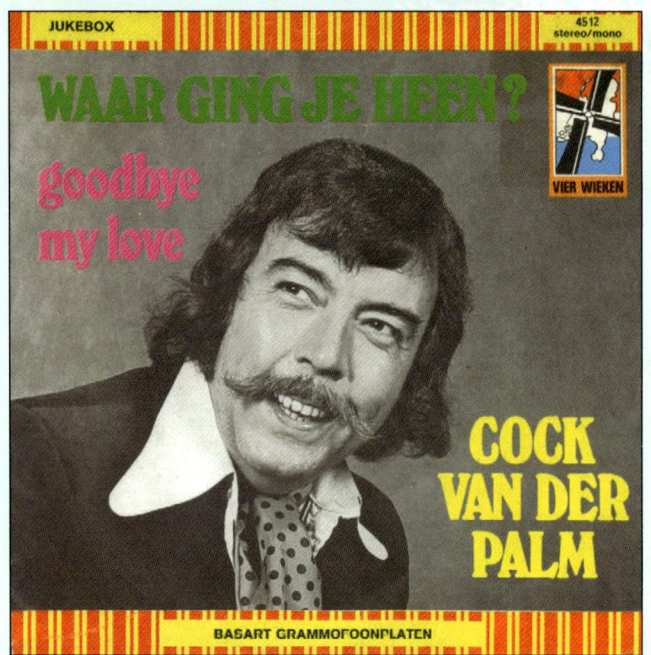

### Cock Van Der Palm • Waar Ging Je Heen?
Vier Wieken / Holland / 1973 7" single

Or "Cocky" to his friends… If you don't know why we have included this then you're obviously reading the book outside the UK; Brits still cannot resist a bit of double entendre. It's just a shame Sid James and the team are not still in business, as Carry On Up The Windmill has missed a character name here. Most of his records feature a jolly photograph of Mr. Van Der Palm on the cover, but despite a lengthy career which began on vinyl in 1962 and continued well into the CD age, a British chart entry somehow eluded him.
That's him in the funny hat bottom left too.

### Kingsize Dick • Letzte Naach
Odeon EMI / 1980 / Germany

Again while the sleeve is not a jaw-dropper, the name just might be. German schlager singer Heinz Ganss' other career choice was as a lumberjack, and apparently Dick is German dialect for an oversize person. When someone explained that he would be known as king size in the UK (where he worked for a time), he put two and two together, ensuring his place in strange vinyl cover listings for the rest of his days. The sleeve with him in the bath also deserves a mention, as nobody has knees that hairy… We should also give an honourary mention to Bill van Dijk, a Dutchman who *"can't wait long"* according to this early 45, and fellow Dutchman Wally Tax, if only as it sounds like something enacted by short time comedy UK Prime Minister Liz Truss's financial wizard. Last but clearly not least is Huug Kok, though he selfishly only recorded as half a Dutch duo, and left no sleeves for us to poke fun at. Trust us, we've looked!

# BIZARRE

## PRIVATELY PRESSED

**Wild Oates • Wild Oates**
SRT / UK
*Photography by T Galvin, AIIP Montgomery, Huddersfield*

Today anyone can upload an audio file to the web and be heard by as many people as their social media reach reaches. In the olden days, DIY meant either duplicated cassettes or, if you gigged regularly, labels who offered a bespoke low run pressing and sleeve service for an all in price, which you could then hopefully sell to fans at shows. SRT in Cambridgeshire were one of the best such labels, producing hundreds of strange and idiosyncratic records which have their own dedicated collectors today. The often bizarre (intentionally or otherwise) cover photos are part of the fun. Which brings us to the Wild Oates, who do a sort of Wilson and Keppel without the Betty (or indeed the sand) tribute act across the cover. . .

The trio, Big Mick Walter on drums (he's the short one), bassist Colin Roberts and Glen Forrest, were based in Huddersfield and did a comedy music act around the clubs of West Yorkshire in the late Seventies (though Colin did cut a real punk single on the side), issuing two albums along the way, with covers clearly intended to make us smile.

Big Mick continues to carve himself a busy career on stage and screen from Blackadder to Green Wing (two of my favourite TV shows of all time) as well as cinema.

**Paul Jones & Set Callé • L'homme Au Violon Bleu**
Bonanza Records 1977 Canada
*Photo / studio production and arrangements: Denis Champoux*

Paul is a Canadian (Québec) fiddler and because of his unusual instrument was often known as L'homme au violon bleu. He could just have easily become known as the man with the daft knitted hat, fluffy slippers and creaky rocking chair given this sleeve (surely the only one ever to feature oven gloves?). And he added levitation to his talent base judging by the cover of his follow up album (left). Bonanza specialised in Canadian interest albums for people who couldn't be bothered to learn English.

Their label logo might warrant an inspection by the woke police brigade too...

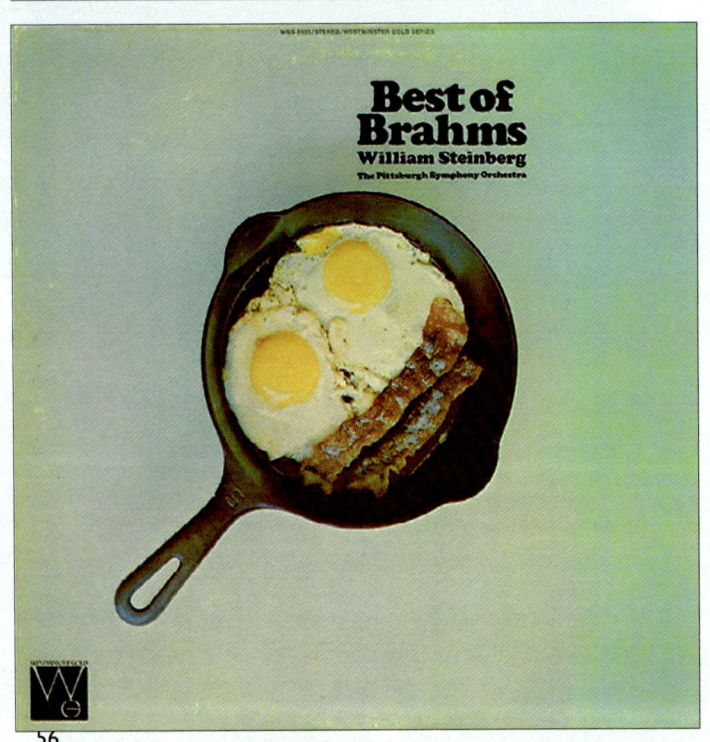

# CLASSICAL CAPERS

### Jean Pierre Jumez • The Nimble Fingers Of
Westminster Gold / USA / 1973
*Designer Christopher Whorf*

Looking to up their classical sales, Westminster, a staid American label bought out by ABC, let designer Christopher Whorf loose, giving the catalogue a remarkably strange yet eye-catching make-over which ran from 1970 up to 1975. The sleeves still resonate with collectors to this day and two made Gramophone's top 15 "Record covers from hell" feature in 2017, including the number one slot. I suppose you either get Whorf's concept right away or scratch your head. Or do both. Yet while this strange sleeve looks totally crazy to us today, seen in context it fits right in. Plus people are still looking at it fifty years after it was created, and there are very few Jean Pierre Jumez albums we can say that of. There appears no reason for the trouserless image other than Whorf thought it might be fun, and it is. Plus the image works against the 'nimble fingers' to create a visual tension. Whether all this attention on the sleeves had an impact on sales we don't know, but are tempted to say 'who cares?'! Steve credits this cover with inspiring his exhibitions: *"This was the record where I decided to make my collection public, when an old friend of mine laughed at this more than I'd ever seen her laugh before!"* We sort of understand **The Planets**, well known to collectors of exotica it changes hands for real money today, being surreal, spacey and sexy all at the same time, but the fried breakfast and frozen cutlery go right over our heads, while the Trans Suez airlines bag full of sausage would have you thrown into jail by either country today.

### RCA Releases 100 Best Melodies

NEW YORK –RCA Records has released a 10-album series, "The 100 Melodies the World Loves Best," with 10 complete melodies in each album as part of RCA's "Summer Sales Power" campaign.

The series is introduced by a one-record sampler containing a few seconds from the theme of each of the melodies titled "Guess That Tune."

Announcement was made by Peter Munves, director of Classical Music, RCA Records, who said: "These are the hundred best known, most often whistled tunes in the classical repertoire... works which have been adapted as popular songs, works which have become famous in film and TV scores and radio themes, and TV commercials."

Munves noted that the sampler album, to be sold at a special low price, was designed for classical radio station guessing game programs and that many stations already planned to program the sampler. He said a special mailing to 240 radio stations with classical programming had been made, and that there would be special mounted display covers, mobiles and other promotion pieces. The albums will ship to dealers in special 60-count display cartons.

### V/A • 100 Great Melodies The World Loves Best Vol 4
RCA Red Seal / USA / 1973

Dating back to the 1940s, RCA Red Seal specialised in classical music. In 1973 they raided their archives for ten albums performed by American orchestras. And slapped an East European bag lady on the front of *Volume 4*! Quite who they figured would impulse buy this, only R. Peter Munves, director of Classical Music at RCA then, could tell us. Munves was a very successful record industry man who loved bringing classical music to the masses, and liked to do things differently. With a background as both a record collector and working in a record shop, in 1971 he pushed RCA's classical sales by 40% just eight months into his new job. *"I'm gonna live to see the day when we wrap a classical album in the same (sort of) package with the Jefferson Airplane,"* he told Billboard magazine. The image was actually shot at the Paris flea market; the rest of the series featured documentary images from around the world; an Indian snake charming, an African girl with a bowl of fruit on her head and a Scotsman in a kilt. RCA even issued a sampler with 100 clips from the set for DJs to use as a radio quiz.

### Pado & Co • Pado & Co
Malligator / France / 1978
*Photo by L. Wiame. Concept by Creac. Stylism by C. Noël*

Concept? Get your trousers off and watch the birdie... maybe it was a play on the last track *Flying Free*. Perhaps Pado (aka Christian Padovan) was inspired by the cover of our *Nimble Fingers* guitarist on the previous page. Otherwise we just have to explain it away as 'being French'. The man behind it was the prolific disco producer, writer and performer Carrone, who perhaps took a chance on this solo album (Malligator was his own label), but it was Pado's last.

*An RCA Red Seal Treasury*

ORMANDY • LEINSDORF • FIEDLER • MARTINON • DOMINGO • MILNES

ARL1-0224 STEREO

# 100 Great Melodies the World Loves Best
## Volume 4

Pomp and Circumstance March No. 1 • A Midsummer Night's Dream: Scherzo • Andante cantabile
Humoresque-Swanee River • Rhapsody in Blue (Main Theme) • The Love for Three Oranges: March
Tritsch-Tratsch Polka • Handel's Largo • Hora Staccato • Ode to Joy (Excerpt)

PHILADELPHIA ORCHESTRA • CHICAGO SYMPHONY • BOSTON SYMPHONY • BOSTON POPS

**Eddie Barclay • Surprise Party!**
Mercury / USA / 1957
*Photo by Don Bronstein*

Not exactly classical but on a strangeness scale it is right up there. French music producer, label owner and band leader Édouard Ruault popped over to America in the early Fifties to take a look at the new LP format, and ended up distributing them in Europe.

By 1957 the American labels were moving to full colour sleeves but why they chose this photograph of who knows what remains a mystery. As Steve says *"it's the contrast between the lettering (which is upbeat) and the three miserable characters. Why the scowls? Why has one got a huge carrot on his nose? Why does the one on the right look like he's praying?"*

Starting out at Playboy, photographer Don Bronstein had a prolific sleeve career considering he died at just 42 but few come up quite as crazy as this. He was a documentary photographer as well so maybe snapped this on one of his assignments, saw the word 'party' in the Mercury brief and thought this would work...

**Chadwick • Symphonic Sketches**
Mercury / USA / 1962 (1958 right)
*Photograph Hugh Cecil Lancelot Bell*

Exactly what inspired this we don't know. It was taken by Caribbean-born jazz photographer Bell, possibly his interpretation of the Hobgoblin piece on this classical collection? Bell's work appeared on jazz albums of the Fifties and Sixties (and he took the Man From Shaft soundtrack photo). Looking more like a Killing Joke album it may have been inspired by Bell's work photographing theatre and dance productions. And talking of mad 'hair'....

**Živan Sazamandié**
Jugoton / Yugoslavia / 1982

*"Živan, when we suggested you had you hair styled for the cover shoot..."* We're not sure if this is a ceremonial hat, strange military headgear, a mad wig or simply a really bad hair day. Either way it just looks very strange on an album, even for a state run label. Živan was a bass singer but only issued three albums (this one was traditional Serb folk material), maybe they ran out of goat hair...

# PERFORMING SEALS

### Riot • Narita
Capitol / UK / 1976
*Cover painting Steven Weiss. Art direction Marcia Loeb*

Just what is meant to be going on here has baffled science for many years. A seals head. On a red sumo wrestler's body. Holding an axe. And, well, excreting skulls?
US hard rock / heavy metal band Riot formed in the mid-Seventies, a time of growing visual absurdity in the genre which they seemed happy to tap into. The group appear to have been obsessed with baby seal heads from day one, grafted on to various humans across their often remarkably juvenile artwork for years. I thought they were trying to emulate Derek Riggs' personification of Iron Maiden's Eddie mascot but metal expert John Tucker was quick to point out Riot's seal predates Eddie. Riot guitarist Lou A. Kouvaris was asked about their *Rock City* debut (left) but seems not to have an answer; the seal becoming a mascot was just a *"random"* happening. He did add that the cover was done by one of the producer's family, always a risky move: *"Hey dad, I got A for art this semester, let me have a go..."* Maybe he gave them mates' rates and as he went on to do the next four sleeves, the band must have loved them.
*Narita* was their follow up, the title and art inspired by riots in Japan trying to stop the expansion of Narita airport (but also took in Stonehenge, an alien, a burning office block and the New York skyline). It made the top ten 'worst metal sleeves of all time' poll at Noisecreep in 2009, Carlos Ramirez suggesting *"the art department at Capitol Records must have been out of their collective minds. Riot crafted some blistering records throughout their three-decade-long discography, but you would be hard pressed to find anyone on the planet that digs the cover."*
Mind you look what they came up with for a Live CD Box Set in Brazil recently (below), words fail us. I shall return my BA to Manchester Polytechnic School of Graphic Design forthwith.

# GLAM GONE WRONG

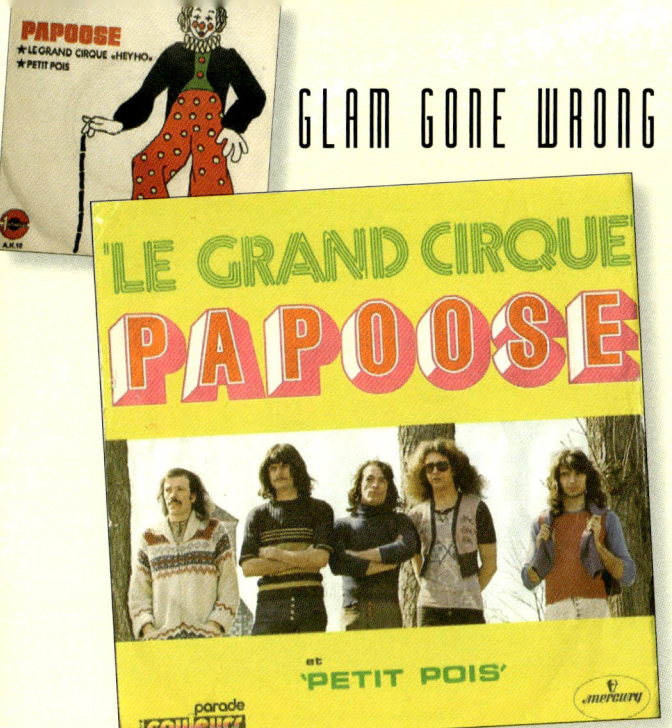

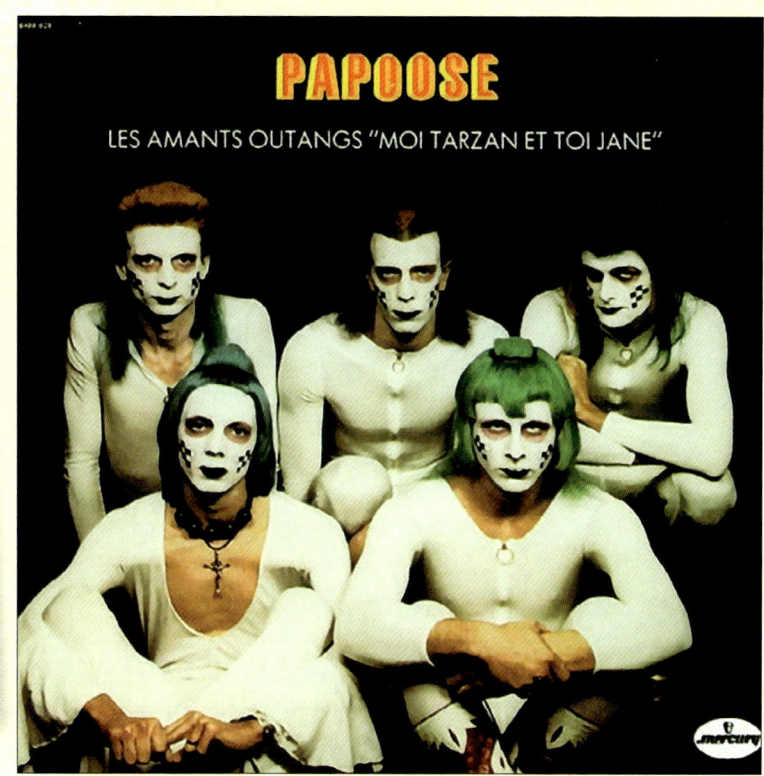

**Papoose • Le Grand Cirque (Hey Ho)**
Mercury / France / 1972
*Photo Claude Delorme*

Who even knew the French embraced glam rock so enthusiastically? Although for embraced, here perhaps read 'jumping on a bandwagon', if the two very different versions of this single are anything to go by: that's the first issue above and the glammed-up version on the left. As we can see, Papoose were a bunch of fairly typical looking hard / prog rock musicians from the early 1970s who suddenly went full-on Sweet. This ill-advised glam look carried over to their one and only album (above right) the following year, with the white make-up and long-johns, and then they disbanded. Cosmetic shops across Paris must have laid staff off.
In Turkey they substituted the terrible sketch of a clown (very top left above). Hey ho indeed. Mind you this label timidness didn't stop everyone there from going glam rock crazy...

**Erkin Koray • Fesuphanallah / Komsu Kizi**
Istanbul Plak / 1971 / Turkey 7" single

Erkin, pioneer of guitar rock in the area (music labelled Turkadelica by some today) and no stranger to dreadful sleeve art, couldn't resist trying the Turkish equivalent of the Boots No. 7 range out just the once with what we might kindly suggest was limited success.

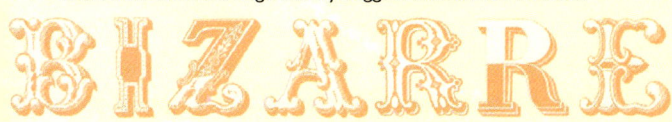

# DISKOS DIVA

**Vera Matovic • Samo Jedan Minut**
Diskos / Croatia / 1987
*Foto I dizajn D. Milovanovic*

Vera had a ton of albums out in Yugoslavia and district following her 1976 debut, all featuring fairly ordinary studio portraits of the lady herself across the years. Then in 1985 she signed to Diskos Records in Serbia, a label not renowned for their cover photographs (check two more bizarre examples of their cover art below).

Diskos likewise quickly lost the plot with Vera, dressing her in OTT Eighties fashions and topping them with strange hair dos. The craziest Diskos sleeve is the one left, *Samo Jedan Minut (Just One Minute)*, where poor Vera looks to be auditioning for the part of a visiting alien space envoy on *Buck Rogers*, but with eye make-up courtesy Worzel Gummidge's fancy piece Aunt Sally. However the mad hair on *Samo Za Tebe Zivim* (above right) comes a close second, hair looking like the photos of the early nuclear bomb tests. Vera also sings on the bewildering 7" with the sheep on (right), goodness knows what that was about. Serbia's entry for Eurovision?

Vera soon went back to her previous label in Yugoslavia and everything calmed down once again.

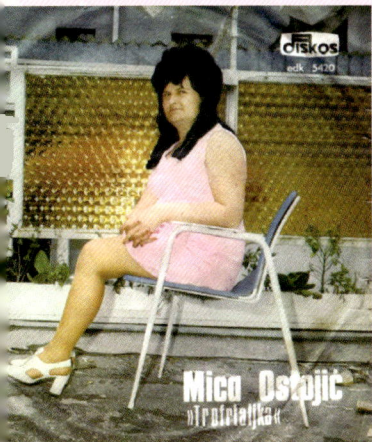

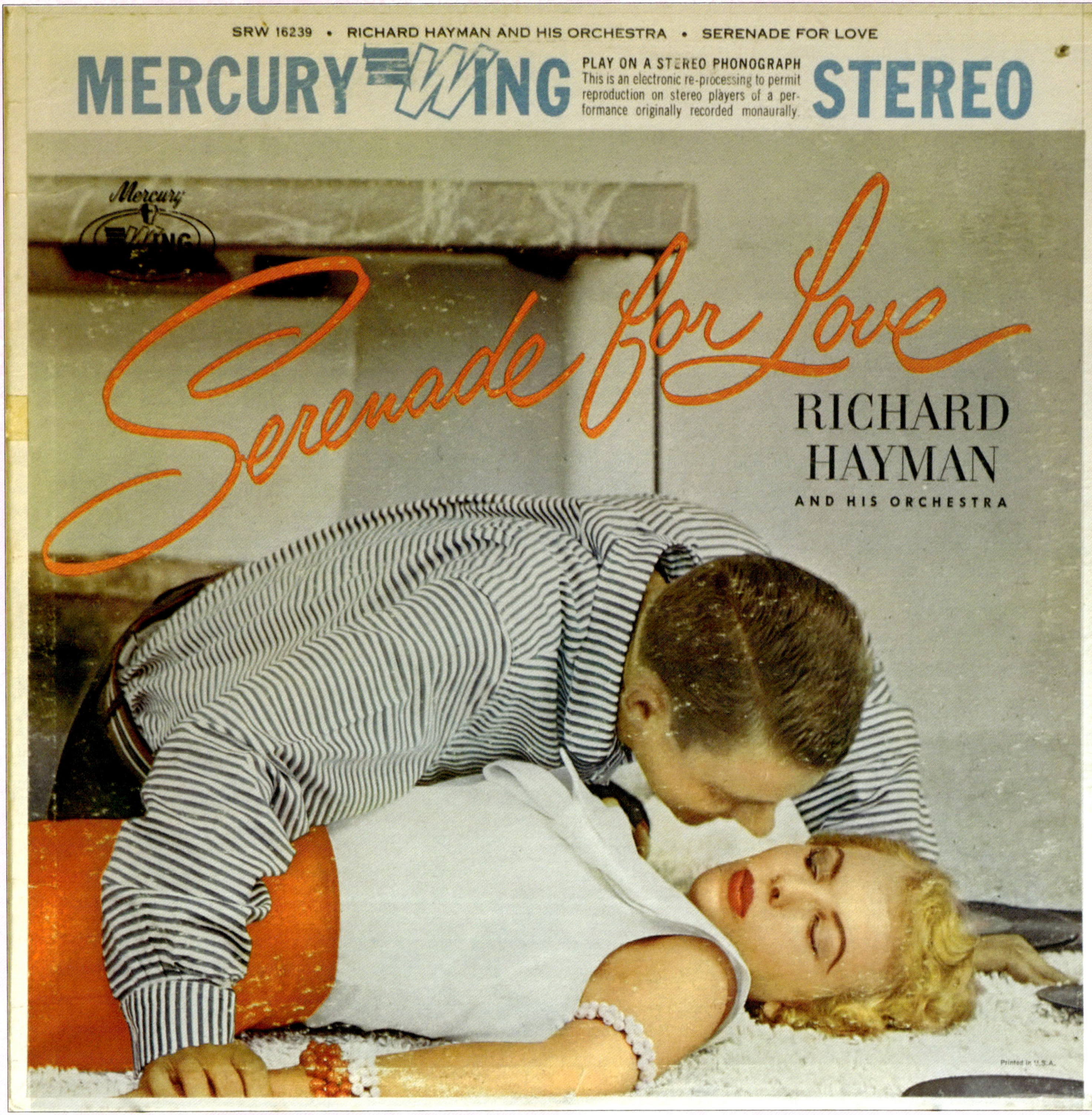
SRW 16239 • RICHARD HAYMAN AND HIS ORCHESTRA • SERENADE FOR LOVE
MERCURY WING
PLAY ON A STEREO PHONOGRAPH
This is an electronic re-processing to permit reproduction on stereo players of a performance originally recorded monaurally.
STEREO
Mercury Wing
Serenade for Love
RICHARD HAYMAN
AND HIS ORCHESTRA
Printed in U.S.A.

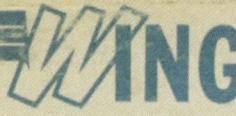

# HASH-TAG METOO

**Richard Hayman And His Orchestra • Serenade For Love**
Mercury Wing / USA / 1963 (first released 1956)

"Seranade for love"? Well fifty years on and despite the goofy bio photo on the back (right), all we can see is what looks like *very* dodgy behaviour indeed. Nobody likes glamorous Fifties sleeves more than I do and you need to make allowances, but most would draw the line at this. I'm not sure what the album on the shag pile (an unfortunate name in the circumstances) is; maybe our unknown cover assailant had just played both sides of Vandermeide's d.i.y *Learn Self-Hypnosis* album to her? There are no design credits.

**Billy May • Cha Cha**
Capitol / USA / 1960

Recorded at the tail end of the 1950s and issued in 1960, May's career was second to none in the quality of his band work, writing, arranging and producing. And generally, unlike many of his contemporaries, he stayed away from exploitative sleeves, so he would probably be horrified at how suspect this image looks today, a priapic older man advancing on a glamorous younger woman (in a remarkable sequin and pink dress) on the dance floor. With a dog under one arm.
It was intended to be a jokey self-deprecating image, just our wokeness today catching up with it. Certainly a previous sleeve, *Plays For Fancy Dancin'*, (above) seems to be pointing up the humour of a man of shorter stature entertaining a more statuesque lady, and is still quite a classic.

69

**STEREO**
PLAYABLE ON STEREO
& MONO PHONOGRAPHS

# BUCK OWENS
### AND HIS BUCKAROOS
# CHRISTMAS SHOPPING

File under: Christmas/Buck Owens

ST 2977

Christmas Shopping
Christmas Time Is Near
Christmas Polka
All I Want for Christmas Is My Daddy
Merry Christmas From Our House to Yours
Good Old Fashioned Country Christmas

One of Everything You Got
Home on Christmas Day
Christmas Schottische
A Very Merry Christmas
It's Not What You Give
Tomorrow Is Christmas Day

## VISIBLE FLAKES

**Buck Owens And The Buckaroos • Christmas Shopping**
Capitol / USA / 1968
*Cover photo Ken Veeder Capitol Photo Studio*

Clearly old Buck needs to put a bottle of Head & Shoulders on the top of that shopping list. The Buckaroos never really managed to break out of America but then they didn't really have to, with over twenty number one hits on the Billboard country charts and even an early *Live In Japan* set in 1967. The LP *Christmas Shopping*, known in the record business as a *"holiday album"*, was a 1968 follow up to a previous Christmas album and just missed the top thirty. Most of his albums went with a similarly wholesome type of cover portrait, though we do like the title of the slightly risque *Buck 'Em* from 1976 and the ill-fitting clobber on his duet with Buddy Alan!

## PRIMARK MOMENT

**Joan Baez • Blowin' Away**
Portrait / USA / 1977
*Cover design and cloud photo John Berg. Cover photo of Joan Kin Schilling*

I would have probably passed this by on a crate digging expedition, but Steve homed in on the absolute absurdity of the cover portrait. Joan, usually very cool looking, dressed in flying goggles giving the camera a wave and a cheesy grin just looks like a real 'we are out of ideas' moment. These or similar silver jackets were all the rage at the time (we bought one at Debenhams and had Neil Murray from Whitesnake try to buy them off us).

You would certainly expect something a little more upmarket for a sleeve by such a major artist. Further confirmation that we were right to include it here came when we found Joan herself dissing the sleeve in a 2017 issue of Rolling Stone, blaming her use of quaaludes in the 1970s for the end result (and in her autobiography describing it as *"a good album with a terrible cover."*)

MCA-519

.MCA RECORDS

**B**ing **C**rosby | "When Irish Eyes Are Smiling"

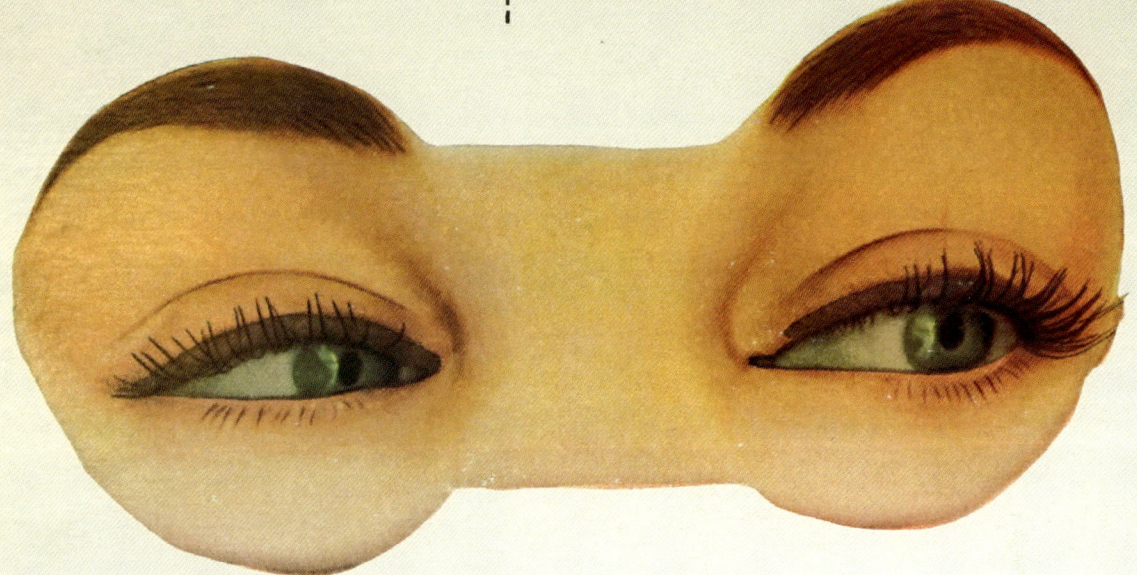

When Irish Eyes Are Smiling
The Rose Of Tralee
Galway Bay
*and others*

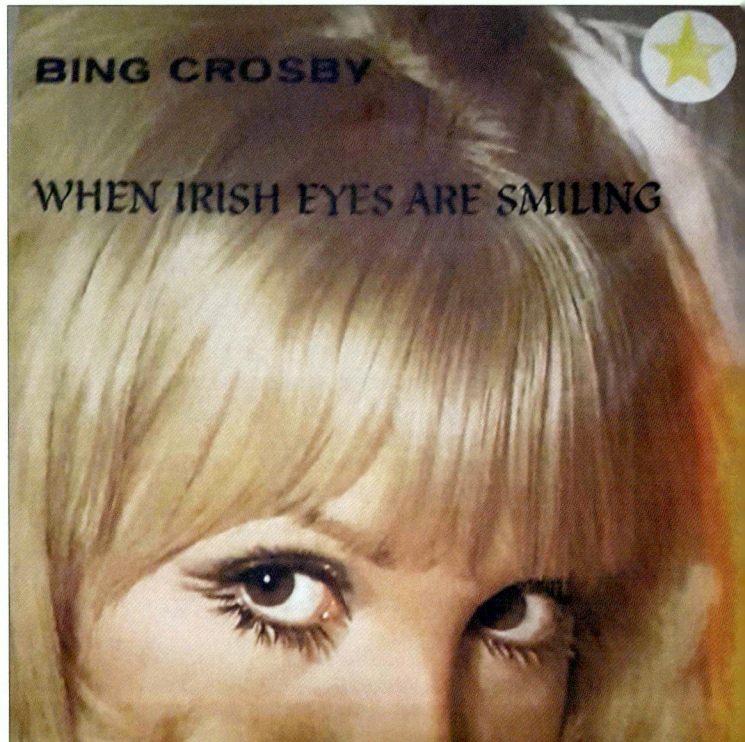

### Bing Crosby • When Irish Eyes Are Smiling
MCA / USA / 1956

A confusing and at times slightly freaky cover. Confusing as it began life on Decca in 1950 as a set of 7" singles, was reissued as a 10" album (with covers featuring a head shot of Bing, a scattering of shamrock leaves and cheap Fifties lettering), then reappeared as a 12" album with those weird disembodied b-movie poster eyes. Softened at the edges to begin with, it looked very awkward. New Zealand tried replacing it with a painting, which merely ended up looking like a cheap cosmetic advert. Finally MCA in America reissued it in 1973 which is when the really awful variation on page 73 emerged, like a cut-out party mask off the back of a cornflake box, lacking only holes for a rubber band. MCA Australia took one look and hastily replaced this with the sultry-ish portrait bottom right, which is probably the look they should have gone with twenty years before. Mind you Bing suffered indignities on a number of sleeves, check *El Senor Bing* on top right... Too-Ra-Loo-Ra-Loo-Ral indeed!

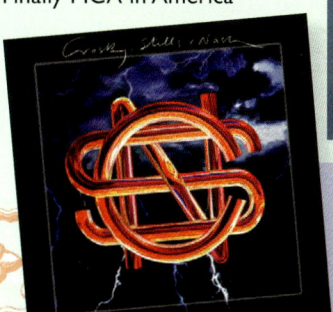

### Crosby Stills Nash • Live It Up
Atlantic / USA / 1990
*Jimmy Wachtel, Art Direction; Sarajo Frieden, Artwork (logo); David Peters, finished artwork*

Most of us think of CSN as hippies stood around outside log cabins, so this bizarre montage (credited to no fewer than three people) from their later reunion is quite a surprise. The back is equally strange, with Nasa astronauts on the moon ... visiting a hot dog stall. It was by all accounts a half-hearted album anyway (Steve being a braver man than me confirms this) and the cover perhaps reflects that, a sort of poor man's Hipgnosis montage which probably meant something to someone at the time but just looks astonishingly naff today. Despite getting its own credit the logo didn't last beyond this, although the next, for *After The Storm,* (inset above) was *really* awful!

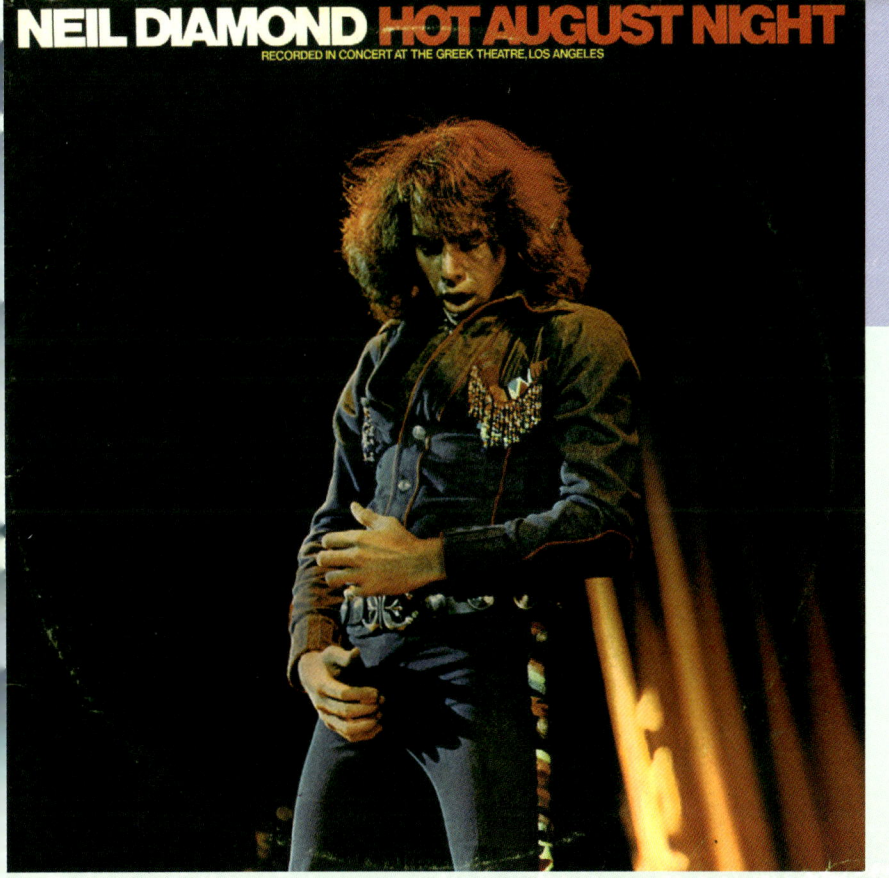

### Neil Diamond • Hot August Night
MCA Records / UK / 1972.
*Art direction George Osaki.*

What a shame Viz magazine called a halt on their 'defacement competition'! This photo (we think it was by Ed Caraeff but others are also credited on the sleeve which has lots of live snaps) is asking for someone with a bottle of tippex to have a go. Needless to say Steve is not the only person to spot this, Lester Bangs got there first in his contemporary review for Rolling Stone: *"He's pantomiming whanging his clanger, and from the look on his face I'd say he's about to shoot off, and the only bogus part is that he'd like everybody out there to think it's 13 inches long."* Jimmy Kimmel asked Neil about the sleeve on ABCTV in 2010 but he coyly claimed he chose the cover as he liked the way it showed off how much hair he had!

# SAUSAGE TIME

*We promise that the idea of a section devoted to sausages on sleeves never occured to us when we began this book. Blame CSN! Vegetarians look away now...*

**Bill Doggett • Hot Doggett**  King Records / USA / 1957

Bill's LP was first issued with a tasteful sketch of the man himself on the cover. Then, possibly inspired by track 1 side 2, *Percy Speaks*, was quickly repackaged in this brash looking sleeve. Love the hand-drawn titling though...

**Wishdokta • Bannana Sausage**
Kickin' Records / UK / 1992 12" single
*Design by Offbeat, Illustration by Junior Tomlin*

For which we can find no excuse, beyond Grant Nelson (aka Witch Doctor) wanting a spoof of Andy Warhol's *Velvet Underground* classic for his early breakbeat single.

**Lou Donaldson • Hot Dog**  Blue Note / USA / 1969
*Photography, Art Direction Frank Gauna*

Even normally classy Blue Note get in on the act! Good photo, rubbish design from the usually great Frank Gauna.

**V/A • Best Known Overtures Volume Two**
ABC Westminster Gold / USA / 1974
*Design Peter Whorf*

Another one from the mad Westminster Gold catalogue seen earlier in the book. Quite why the devil is looking so affronted by his rather lacklustre looking hot dog isn't clear, or indeed why it adorned this compilation for the label in the first place.

**Jomfru Ane Band • Rock Me Baby**
Aman / Denmark / 1978
*Forside cover Ole Halfdan.*

Named after a theatre in their home town apparently... The air-brush is a difficult piece of equipment to master and clearly Ole had only just begun to get to grips with it on this illustration, or was he distracted by erotic thoughts while at the drawing board? What else might account for the game of pocket billiards the gentleman seems intent on, or indeed the large phallic Danish sausage? And all to very little effect if the bride's face is anything to go by. Ole did at least a dozen record sleeves, every one of which was much better than this!

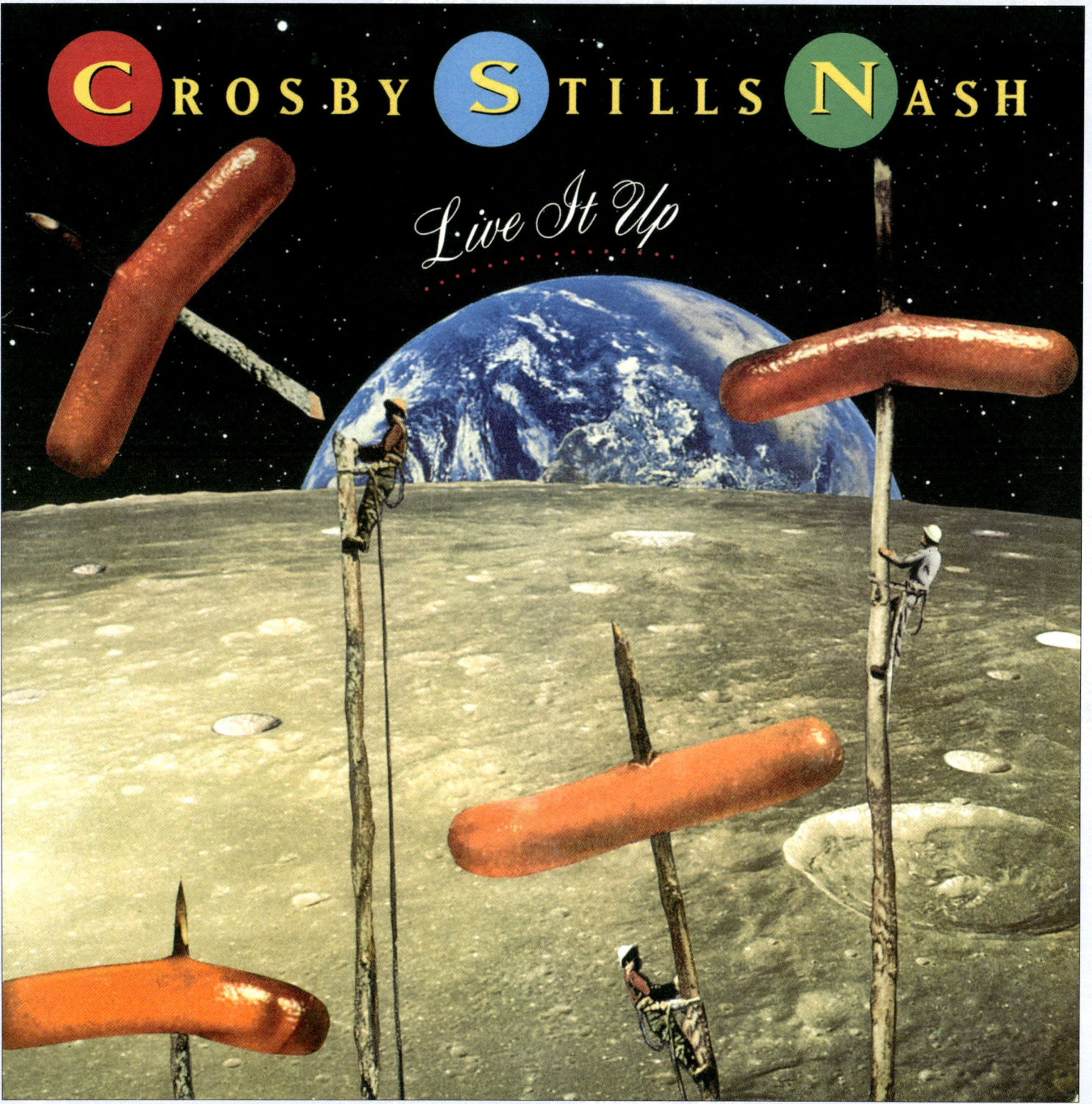

# JOMFRU ANE BAND
## Rock me Baby

# MEHTOO MOMENT

**Olivia Rodrigo • Sour**
Geffen / Germany / 2021
*Thank you to Kirsten Stubbs, Marissa Romirez and Christiana Dirona for helping me to bring Sour to life visually.*

Meh might have been a better title. Olivia loves the environment one minute and then issues her debut album on ELEVEN different colours of vinyl, four different coloured plastic CD cases, the same number of cassette versions plus an alternate sleeve as well.

Cover wise it seems like nobody even thought about vinyl as the image looks like it was enlarged from a CD, while the confected rebel image is so artificial it makes Generation X look like the real deal. Still with a number one across several countries the record label must be happy. And at almost £50 for a pair of branded jogging trousers made who knows where, the merchandisers likewise. It says a lot that the store menu comes before the music one on the website too!

**Tex Morris and The Ranchers • Way Out West**
Fidelio / UK / 1962
*Illustration Y.E.E.B*

How very bona. Fidelio, an unabashed budget label, was owned by William Barrington Coupe, jailed in 1966 for passing off recordings he didn't own. And then resurfaced nearly 40 years later to do it all over again on CD, claiming stolen piano recordings issued on his revived label were all by his wife!
Tex Morris and The Ranchers may be a bunch of session players, or the label could simply lifted some obscure American country tracks and made the name up. The sleeve illustration (which also turned up on a children's EP) is gauche in the extreme, looking like the dust-jacket from some sort of amateur Fifties gay western pulp novel (though the rope lettering is fantastic).
For some unknown reason Fidelio also issued the album in a different illustrated cover which is just as amateur. This version is signed Y.E.E.B and the two covers may be by the same artist. Y.E.E.B did a few more gaudy covers for the label, including two musicals, then vanished.

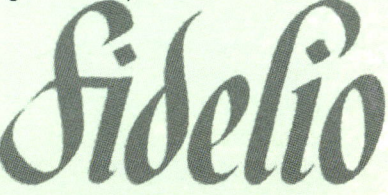

# Way Out West

*Fidelio*

CYM 76902
STEREO

# The Kaye Family

CYMRU RECORDS

The Recording Company of Wales

# YOU CAN'T PICK YOUR FAMILY

**The Kaye Family • The Kaye Family**
Cymru Records / Wales / 1972
*Photography Richard Hammonds and Eric Beard*

"It gives us great pleasure to be with you in sound whilst you are sitting in your favourite comfortable armchair listening to us…"

…and playing with your giant felt rodent while you do so! By all means get spruced up for your album photo shoot but who thought those uncuddly toys were a good idea? The Kaye Family were a mum-and-dad duo who added their two children to the mix as soon as they were old enough (sonny boy on an impressive double bass drum kit a la Cozy Powell, though Cozy's didn't feature two saxophones strapped to the front as far as I can remember).
There are some reviews out there which suggest the awful sleeves actually put people off and some feel the performances are fairly decent if bland, so next time one of these turns up in your local charity shop maybe give it a try. I say 'next time', I have spent years crate digging and never seen one. They had the audacity to cover Telstar by The Tornados too, I'm dying to hear that.
The live album (below left) ended their vinyl career in 1974, but is reckoned to be sub-bootleg quality and again we've never found a copy of this either.

**The Singing Nolans**
Nevis / UK / 1972

If you want the ultimate family snashot you can't go wrong with The Nolans first LP, issued on a small indie label. There were so many Nolans at this time the cameraman had to balance one on top of the wall to fit them all in. Surely the most white vinyl thigh boots on a record sleeve ever? Chart smashes followed six years on, once the sisters dropped the fellers!

# HE'S MORE THAN JUST A SWEAR WORD

**Dave Boyer • Just Because I Asked**
Word Records / USA / 1975
*Sleeve photograph Eric Skipsey*

*"My first priority as a servant of Jesus Christ..."* was clearly not to employ a sleeve designer. Dave has been thanking the Lord for over two dozen albums and CDs (Website Special: *'All 7 Dave Boyer CDs for only $77.00 plus postage, a $105 value'*). Mostly the covers are just Dave and those teeth, or sometimes (as left) Dave, his wife and child and *their* teeth, and they regularly make 'strange sleeve polls'. These sort of Amateur Photographer style double exposure portraits rarely come out well, here it just looks like a darkroom mistake / medical experiment (just why is one head so much smaller than the other?) involving conjoined twins. American christian jazz singer and gospel artist Boyer did most of his albums for religious labels like Word (*'The finest name in sacred music'*) and Reverence, and you could still book him to sing at your event as recently as 2022; just don't expect any Little Richard covers.

The photographer did lots more covers for Word, as well as pop acts such as The Righteous Brothers, and most are a lot better than this. Though we hope he took out public liability insurance when snapping Gloria Roe's hair-do here...

**Larry Orell • Larry Orell**
Hymntime Records / USA / 1973

*He's More Than Just A Swear Word.* And we know that thanks to a track on this album, where multi-tasking Southern gospel singer, minister and life coach Larry also stops a willow tree from falling over while simultaneously modelling oversize clothes for the Sears summer catalogue.

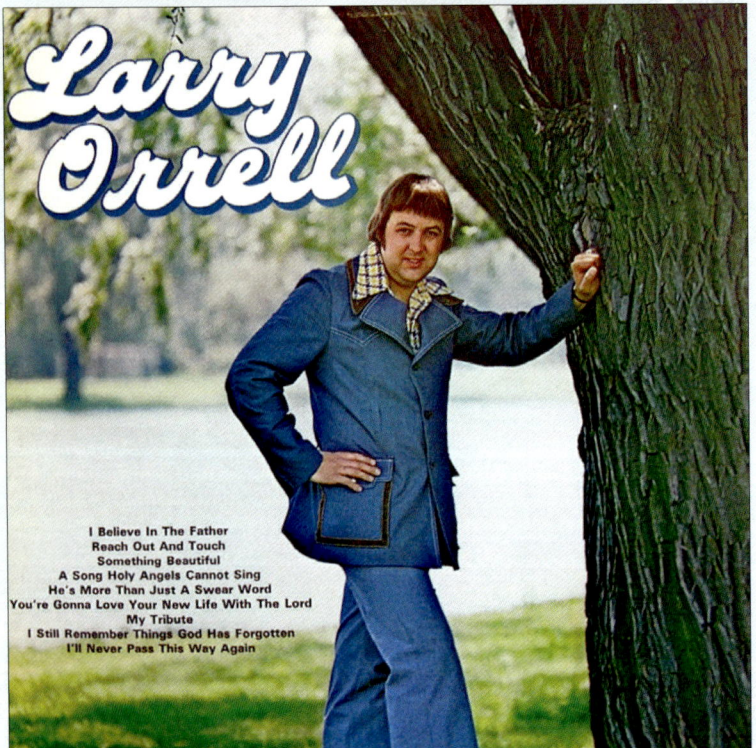

# HE'S MORE THAN JUST A SWEAR WORD

## BOULEVARD

**V/A • Godspell**
Boulevard / UK

Let's not beat about the bush here. Boulevard (launched by Allied Records, owners of downmarket labels including Society, Presto and Saga) was without doubt the budget label other budget labels looked down on, with product racked out in the wire dump-bins of Spar (hello to all the sexists at the counter in our local branch) and Mace grocers, the ultimate example of records as product.

No unnecessary expense was incurred in the production or development of the catalogue and certainly no real thought given to the repertoire whatsoever. Given all this, the cheap cover for their recording of *Godspell* starts to make sense.

In 1971, their first year of operation, Boulevard pushed out 70 albums at random, each selling for less than 50p. Which is about what it looks like this sleeve cost to design. Using sheets of Letratint (a sort of posh sticky-backed see-through film printed with various dot screen sizes), this is without doubt a dreadful piece of graphic design, rendered in two colours to save money at the printers. The back just has an illustration of Jesus cut out of an old book and enlarged.

Boulevard albums filled the charity shops in the 1990s but have now more or less vanished as the generation who bought them now passes on. A couple of their records are even worth serious money; *Godspell* isn't one of them.

**Marigold • Marigold**
Skylite / USA / 1978
*Cover design Charles Hooper*

"Vivacious" Marigold Cheshier looks like she has been propped up after a good night out while her friends hunt for a taxi. Skylite are a wonder of a religious label, documented on a site dedicated to *"preserving the legacy of Southern gospel music"*. Started in 1959, it was taken over by Joel Gentry in 1966, but things went downhill in later years as the banks auctioned off his interests and Joel was convicted for armed bank robbery. Anyone looking for remastered CD editions is going to be disappointed too as their master tape store was attacked in suspected arson attacks. Twice. Someone wasn't a fan. Still the label left lots more covers to astonish, four of which are overleaf. There are **The Rebels Quartet** (a five piece) who all fell asleep in the early Sixties while Grandfather read stories from the bible to a turkey (and later went up in an atomic blast!), plus some great Eithties hair-dos courtesy **The Masters Five**. Not to mention **The Speer Family**; any relation to our Albert?

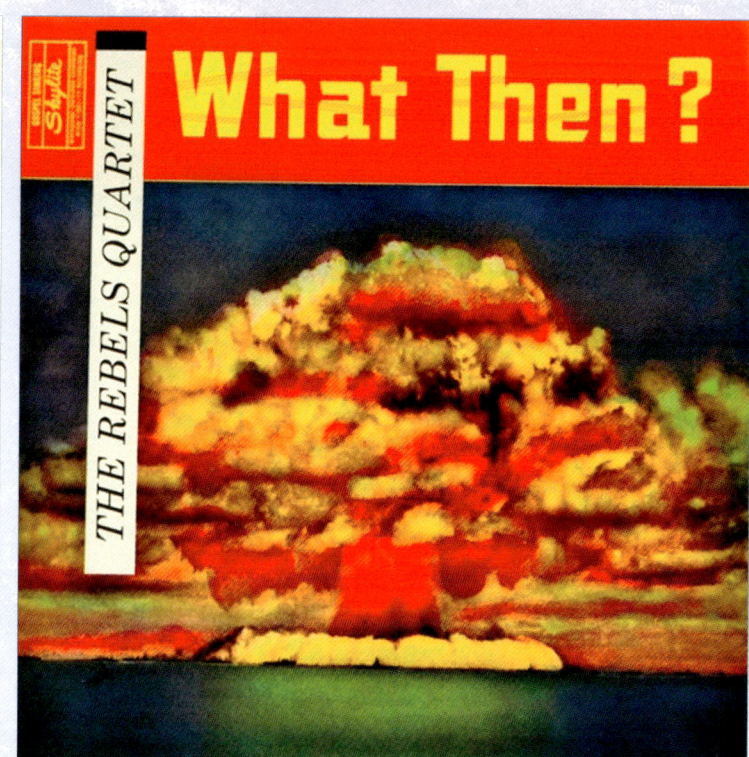
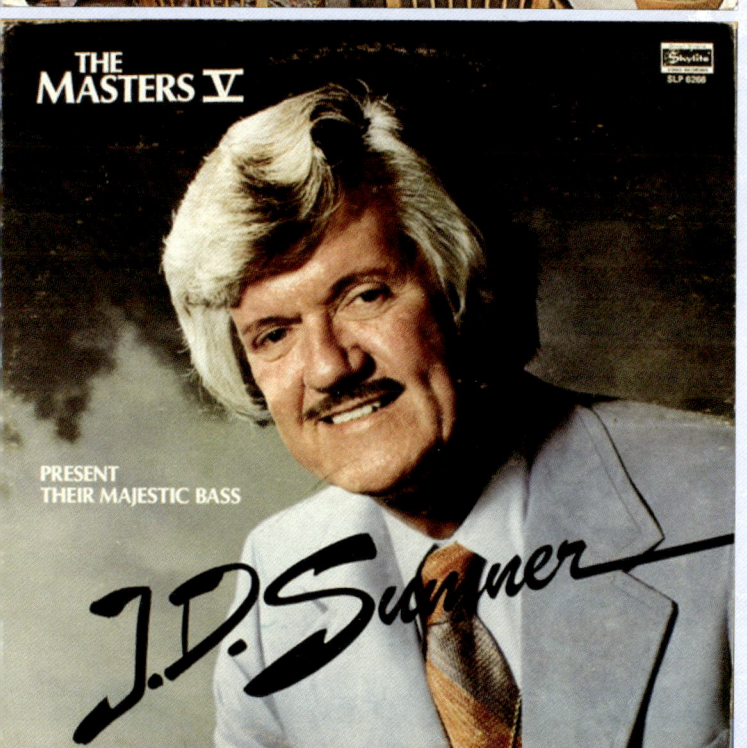

# HE'S MORE THAN JUST A SWEAR WORD

**Mike Adkins • Thank You For The Dove**
self released [no pun intended]

With no label, one assumes Mike probably sold these albums direct at his ministries. But the more you look at this cover, the more you see Mike about to sink his teeth, Ozzy style, into the poor old dove. We presume it was already dead and this is a studio set up (check out the carefully daubed background foliage). And as with most of these religious albums, the harder the effort to look super sincere for the camera, the less convincing it all becomes.

Mike can then be seen going through the bible with a marker pen on the front of *Lord Of All*, marking up all the good bits, and this highlighting work can then clearly be seen on the next album *He Is Near*, along with a pair of zip-up boots (I thought Jesus always wore sandals)... and a trumpet. We still haven't figured that one out, or indeed exactly where Mike has blasted off to.

For any rock fans, this LP opens with a track called *Stargazer*, and I idly wondered if this was a cover of Ritchie Blackmore's metal masterpiece? Steve says not. Shame.

## Aage Samuelsen • Jeg Synger Hoyt Av Glede
EMI / Norway / 1981  *Foto Terje Engh*

Nor did the Americans have the holier than thou vinyl market sewn up. Here comes Aage from Norway, albeit looking more geriatric-spooky-magician than benign preacher (he was only 65 when this photo was taken). And there's that dove again; maybe there is an evangelical animal trainer hiring them out for cover shoots, though on the back (right) Aage looks like he's about to twat the poor thing off his bible.

After being booted out of the church (for faith healing rather than cruelty to animals), Aage speedily founded his own religious movement, but once more began to slide; it was found that the collection money was being spent at the off-license rather than on missionary works. He then somehow managed to swing a deal with EMI Norway in 1979 and began churning out long players, often two or three a year. We especially like the one below right where on first glance it seems Aage (now looking like a John Lithgow tribute act) has so inspired one member of the church that he has whipped off his hair-piece in the excitement of it all.

## Denny Strand • Gentle Spirit
Rainbow / USA

Another one going for the dove look, though Denny does seem like he's worried about this one letting go over his hand, though most of us can see it is very obviously fake. Full marks for the dapper outfit though, less so for the dreadfully unreal studio backdrop.

# Aage Samuelsen
## Jeg synger høyt av glede

8 C 062-37424
STEREO

# HE'S MORE THAN JUST A SWEAR WORD

**Tommy Ellison • Let This Be A Lesson To You (Drunk Driver)**
Air Records / USA / 1985 ☞

*"Alcohol and gasoline do not mix!"*
So explains the Rev. Larry McCollough, in case you missed the point with that cover, looking like a scene from the set of John Wick. Gospel singer Tommy kicks off with his seven minute opening title track in which a drunk driver kills a little girl, goes to jail, gets out and does it all over again, this time taking out his mother. *"Now directed by the Holy Spirit, Tommy Ellison puts to music the brutality and misery drunk driving inflicts."* You can't argue with the sentiment, though it is a fairly ham-fisted effort all round, another sleeve which raises more questions than answers; exactly why were the two automobiles racing round a graveyard in the first place? What are those brown lines for on the cover? Tommy tries to emote for the cameraman, looking like he's just dropped one of the victim's heads out of his hands. Hollywood casting agents aren't exactly going to be fighting for his number.

**Father Francis • Herald of The King Volume 3**

No label details at all on this weirdo cover. Hailing from the Franciscan Friary in Holywell (not one assumes a silent order), Fr. Francis belts out fifteen suitably zealous performances, so *Fernando* and *Una Paloma Blanca* rock up next to *The Old Rugged Cross*. "Royalties" (the speech marks are his not ours) all going to support missionary work (I know parts of Wales are a little remote but even so...). He's still at it too and to date has done over forty albums, some still available on cassette, for trendy format followers. You can download the full catalogue from his website.
Francis's other claim to fame was his knitting. Specifically the little knitted dolls based on his own image (are we not on theologically dodgy ground there?) which dangle from the neck of his guitar and could be bought to support the cause.
Last time I was working in Amazon studios (where this was cut), they had lots of sleeves on the wall of albums recorded there. This wasn't among them. Shame.

**Jim McKnight • It Is Written**
Rainbow Records / USA

As one wag commented, *"Just point, we'll do the rest."* Thanks to his awkward hunkered down stance it looks like they built up Jim's body from three photographs. Rainbow's LPs are hard to date, but while it looks like something from the Fifties this is actually late 1970s. There is little known about Jim, though this sleeve remains a source of endless online comment. And that's before we get to the little demons, skewered by swords carrying bible references. If only it was that easy eh? Still God loves a trier.

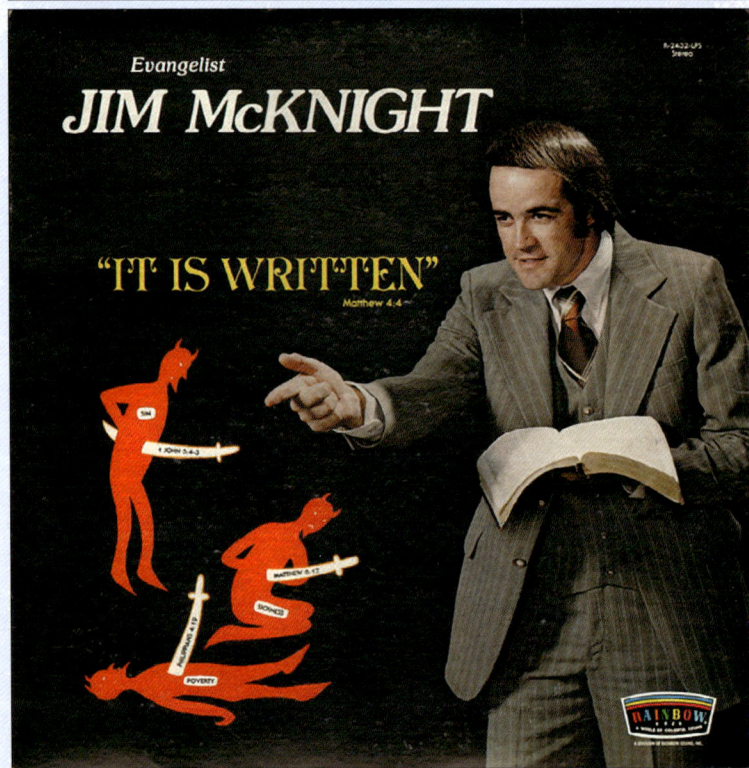

# AN APPLE A DAY

**Jayson Hoover • Jayson Hoover**
Mushroom Records Canada 1974
*Album concept & photography Toby Rankin. Album design Deborah Shackleton (Tony Rankin & Associates). Props and stuff Jacalyn Granbery*

Although Jayson had been on the Canadian music scene since the early Sixties, his band opening for Led Zeppelin and Vanilla Fudge in 1968, this looks to be his only solo album. Issued by Mushroom Records who had just gone big with the group Heart (Tony Rankin was responsible for the photographs on their debut *Dreamboat Annie*), there was the budget for a gatefold sleeve but clearly not for a stand in for Eve, so poor old Jayson (who looks faintly embarrassed by the whole affair) had to make do with a shop mannequin. And a tree of knowledge with no leaves on, plus a toy snake. I wonder who had to bite all the apples too? It's one of those cover concepts which probably sounded OK when they sat around in the Mushroom office, but failed to live up to their vision in the photo studio, by which time the budget had been blown. Curiously the inner gatefold has a much nicer head shot of a woman biting an apple, which would clearly have been a better cover choice.
Issued only in Canada it is quite a rare record today. Steve's copy has clearly been through some hard times but we kind of like this lived in look which tells of fifty years of sitting on people's shelves.
A sticker on some copies suggests the LP contains 'three hit singles', but this proved to be wishful thinking; *She's My Lady* was a top 20 hit in Winnipeg, the others weren't. Too late to ask for a refund.

# TREES TALK TOO

**Geraldine And Ricky • Trees Talk Too!**
World Records / USA

The skill of a ventriloquist lies in convincing an audience that the dummy is talking. Once you move the act to vinyl, well you don't need to be Donald Trump to think there might be some fakery going on. On the other hand, as you have probably already suspended rational thought to take in any form of religious indoctrination, hearing it from the mouth of a wood and plaster dummy is hardly a massive leap of faith.
So let us introduce you to the wide-eyed, creepy (and ever so slightly Michael Jackson-y) Ricky. Details of *Trees Talk Too!* are sketchy (as indeed is the science behind the title, only now catching up with Ricky's ramblings) but there are two alternate sleeves, the splendid jungle portrait on the previous page by Fred Hamby and the rather less fabulous painted cover above which is even rarer (we've not been able to find a copy).
Geraldine Murray claimed God delivered her the gift of ventriloquism while she was asleep at age 14; how did that work? There seems to be a more adult theme than you might think on some tracks too. *He Touched Me* may well predate the MeToo movement, and what *The Liquor Store* is about we hate to think. Like us you probably thought one ventriloquist dummy preaching on vinyl was as good as it gets but no, there are more!

**Geraldine And Ricky • Geraldine And Ricky**
Distributed by Christ For The World Inc. Florida, USA

The pair's debut album (above left) with an almost life-size image of the dummy cosying up to Geraldine was self pressed and seems to be a live recording. Both discs are from the early 1970s.

**Erick And His Manipulator Beverly Massegee • Amen!**  Rainbow / USA / 1974

Looking ever so post-coital on the cover, like Geraldine, Beverly was also doing it all live. Before she began manipulating Erick (stop sniggering), the lady had an event-filled life, from Playboy 'circuit entertainer' (her words not ours), being married to a Dixie mafia hitman and rumoured by some to be The Babushka Lady, untraced witness to Kennedy's assassination. But it is through her two bizarre 1974 albums (above) as a religious vent act that she seems to have found 'worst sleeve' immortality. Recorded at large open air gatherings, they feature rambling twenty minute pieces in which *"Erick never fails to amuse both young and old with his somewhat unconventional views of well-known Bible stories, and his perceptive insights into the lives of the Church and its members."* It's not going to worry Nina Conti. Beverly did record without Erick, mostly religious music (*He Touched Me*) plus a spoken word autobiography, releases now at last available (along with Erick's discs) on CD from the family website, all tax deductable. Bless.

**Do You Know Jesus? • Uncle Les & Aunt Nancy Wheeler**  USA / 1979

This pair (left) followed Erick and Ricky's groundbreaking lead with their dummy who is Randy (it says so on the cover), working *"in the service of the King,"* but only in the Michigan area. Self pressed, and with more of their puppets featured on the back cover, this seems to have been Randy's only vinyl outing. Maybe his hair-care bills got out of hand.
God love the Seventies eh? All this *and* flared trousers.

# JOYEUX NOËL

**V/A • Joyeux Noël**
*Muse / 1969 / Canda*

The Christmas record (welcome or not) has been around at least since the 1940s. Most labels have pushed out a seasonal compilation at one time or another, but a pre-requisite is normally a beaming face or two. Here the cover just drains the onlooker of any festive spirit as our model looks like she's spent ages setting up the tree only for the photographer to appear hours late. After paying for a cover shoot (with arguably the cheapest artificial tree they could find), the label then chose the dullest shot on the roll of film, perhaps confusing bored with sultry (we know this as the cover model changed into a gold lamé outfit for the inner gatefold and can be seen at least trying to smile!). And let's not forget the back cover (top of page 101), dull beyond belief. Yet Muse were so pleased with sales a follow up appeared in 1970 (also next page) after which the label closed. The Christmas vinyl market could really do with a book all to itself, such is the sheer variety of kitsch, cheesy or plain bewildering covers. We have included some of our favourites over the next few pages to support the Canadian diva's offering.

**V/A • Jezus Krisztus Szupersztar**
Pepita Records / 1986 / Hungary
*Grafika es Fotok by Kozma Peter*

Unless you believe in the Turin shroud, we know ALL illustrations of Jesus are by their very nature invented. But on very few does he come over quite as manic as this. Here our tidy-bearded lord and saviour looks like he is being interfered with from behind by something oversized from the adult shop. Hungarian songwriter Miklós Tibor is the man responsible, not for the adult shop purchase, but adapting this Lloyd / Weber classic. He had a go at Evita next, as if the world needed any more versions.

**Merry Cajun Christmas • Volume Two**
Swallow Records

While this looks like something from a local art show in the 1950s, it was released as recently as 1987. The bizarre thing is that *Volume One* had a fairly professional looking cover of snow clad trees, so why they opted for this ham-fisted follow up is beyond us. Mind

you *Volume One* did also have a sketch of Santa and his sleigh pulled by alligators on the back! The artist, Mike Bordelon, did a couple more covers for this Louisiana label which started back in the late Fifties (and is still going strong). I wonder if Santa ever made the perilous journey from boat to shore?

### The Border Brass • Tijuana Christmas
Pickwick Design Records / USA / 1967

A musical style not notably connected with Christmas but which (mainly thanks to Herb Alpert) was very popular in the late Sixties and with budget labels. Here Design Records (something of an oxymoron given their often terrible covers) commissioned this over-enthusiastic cover shoot. The model looks like he is giving himself a hernia (are those, as someone in our office wondered, piles at the end of his trumpet?) trying to play the trumpet with knitted mittens. Nor are we sure what inspired the psychedelic pattern round the edge. In Britain they added some half hearted holly leaves around the title to try and jolly it up. It didn't.

### Kico • Christmas With Kico
Jugoton Records / Yugoslavia / 1983

Kico clearly shares an obvious dread of the season with our *Joyeux Noel* cover star, and looks far from pleased to be photographed made-up like a school janitor on this LP from the state owned label Jugoton. But while the make up artist has done his or her best (the orange moustache and grey distemper on the eyebrows and lashes really set the look off), we would certainly want Kico to take a DBS check before letting him loose in our grotto. Singer Krunoslav 'Kico' Slabinac had a prolific 40 year career in Coatia, covering rockabilly to Slavonian folk but this seems to have been his biggest success (now remastered for CD). But apart from a few times when his national costume might amuse (sorry Croatia, but those lacy trousers do looks suspiciously like Queen Victoria's undergarments) on covers, nothing was as worrying as this.

### Thore Skogman • Klappa På
EMI / Sweden / 1963  *Photograph C.A. Carlson*

Swedish singer and songwriter Thore Skogman is so popular in his own country there is even a museum devoted to him. This 7" single (*Clap On*) clearly has a comedy angle but appears to have pushed the bounds of bad taste too far even for Sweden, and was hastily reissued with a much more cosy photo of him as Santa greeting a little girl. The Swedish version of the infamous Beatles butcher cover? It's enough to give vegetarians nightmares. We've seen better artificial trees too.

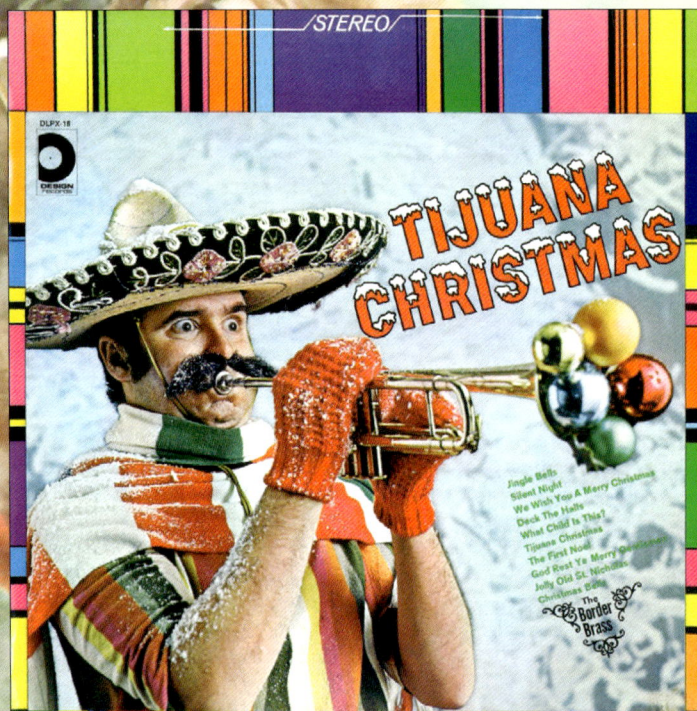

## V/A • May You See Jesus This Christmas
Mustard Seed / Canada / 1984
*Photography Chuck Groot, Old Masters Portrait Studio. Graphic design and Typesetting Alston Graphics. Photographic props Apple-Jo*

Some folk spend their time creating bizarre LP sleeves and slipping them onto the internet where they get picked up and circulated as the real thing. Steve strongly suspected this to be another. But then he found a copy for real. So we somehow need to work out why this gorky bloke is gazing into a manger containing a plastic baby doll in swaddling, with a gift of an empty packet of Players No. 10. The person who assembled these bizarre props even gets a credit for goodness sake.

The album is a collection of poems, religious nonsense and spoken word, and perhaps not surprisingly was The Mustard Seed Church's only release. Once they'd all bought each other a copy for Christmas and that much prayed for break-out hit never happened, they called time on the studio. Mind you the church itself is still out there doing good work by way of foodbanks in Victoria, and we got a good laugh out of the sleeve, so everyone is a winner. Steve has gone the extra mile and actually played it, and tells me it starts with *"Happy birthday to you, happy birthday to you, happy birthday dear Jesus..."*

## Gayla Peevey • I Want a Hippopotamus for Christmas
*Columbia / USA / 1953 78rpm*

Christmas brings out the silly in all of us, so the fact that this went Top 30 in the Billboard charts at the time will surprise nobody. Though why there should be over half a dozen cover versions of it remains less clear.

Apparently the local newspaper started a fund to buy little Gayla a real Hippo, although what they expected a ten year old to do with it we have no idea (just taking it for walkies would be the first logistical challenge).

Gayla continued to issue singles into the early Sixties, retiring at the grand old age of 19 but never got any royalties from this.

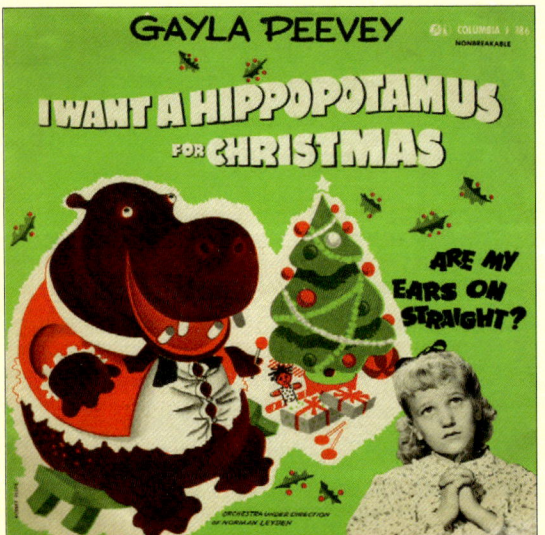

## V/A • A First Christmas Record For Children
Columbia / USA / 1957
*Photos Tom Yee*

Quite an early Christmas album, with the first Columbia logo and graphic in the corner. Where the scary papier-mache Santa mask with the Cross of Lorraine comes in is less certain, he doesn't look that child-friendly to us, just really creepy indeed.

Cameraman Yee did a handful of early Columbia jazz covers but then seems to have moved on to other work.

It was the nightmares probably.

**Slim Whitman • Christmas With**
Epic / USA / 1980
*Photography Bill Barnes. Design Bill Johnson*

Ding dong ladies!
*"Shall I amuse the kids with my Hugh Hefner impression before dinner?"*
*"Probably best just let them open their presents dear. And I hope you've not just given them all a copy of your Christmas album...."*
Sadly though, he has. Who thought this was a good look for the cover? Happily Slim was nothing like this in real life but here comes over as the sort of dodgy louche uncle you would not leave in charge of your teenage daughters while you nipped off to the cinema. Musically it's ten quick knock-offs of everyday carols, cut in Nashville, with details of how to join the Ottis Dewey 'Slim' Whitman Appreciation Society on the back. His country yodelling music is very much an acquired taste but check out the soundtrack of the *Mars Attacks* film, where his yodelling causes the Martian's heads to explode and so save the world. Genius.

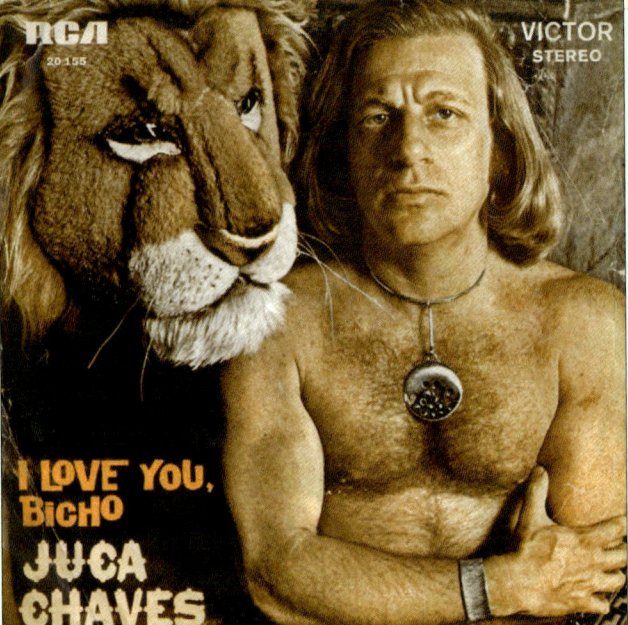

# SEVEN INCH STRANGENESS

**Juca Chaves • I Love You, Bicho**
RCA Victor / Brazil / 1975 7" single

Brazilian beefcake / lion tamer Jurandyr Czaczkes Chaves was certainly not against having a laugh or showing off his impressive torso on record sleeves. But he rather belies this he-man looks on this one, with a life-size stuffed replica of a lion. Even RKO would have baulked at this in the Tarzan films. Still, 18 albums, three dozen singles (his first in the late Fifties), exiled first from Brazil and then Portugal for his anti-military and anti-fascist views, we can forgive him a few duff covers.

**Soulful Dynamics • Dying Snowman**
Mercury / Germany / 1982 7" single

The cheerful group photo here sits very much at odds with the grim title of this funk / soul record, from the German based band (originally from Liberia). It looks like it was their last hurrah as well, after a decade long career. Hardly one you'd wish to buy your kids for Christmas. The bleak Barbara Kruger-esque title strip would ruin most festive occasions and the poor old snowman isn't going to last long under that sun, his cries deadened by the fancy earmuffs they're all wearing...

**V/A • Hand In Hand 8 Gouden Favorieten Voor Het Eerst Op Één Plaat**
Commissie Collectieve Grammofoonplaten Campagne Holland / 1964 / 10" mini album   *Fotos Frits Gerritsen*

Winner of longest title AND record label name in the book, this is just a very odd image, one of Steve's personal favourites. As he points out, it takes time to appreciate just how *Wicker Man* strange it really is. We had no idea who the bloke in the picture frame was, or why the group of tidily clothed Sixties hipsters were walking round with it.
The CCGC was a Dutch record label collective who held an annual contest for local musicians, the prize being a special vinyl release; an X Factor precursor if you will, except everyone is properly dressed. Turns out Gert Timmermans couldn't be bothered to turn up for the cover shoot, so they stuck his mugshot on a frame instead! The CCGC also hosted their own version of the Grammys, The Edisons, starting in 1960 and still going strong, recognising international as well as Dutch artists.

# TRAGEDY

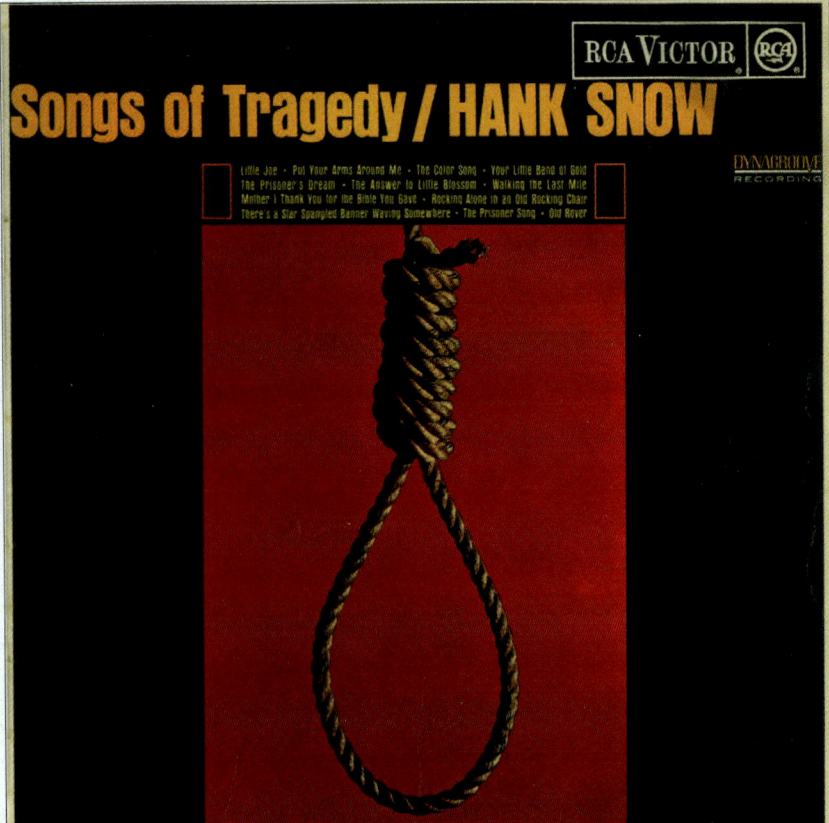

**Hank Snow • Songs Of Tragedy**
RCA Victor / USA / 1964

Hank Snow, the man who introduced Elvis to Tom Parker. Cheers Hank. Even amongst a musical genre *known* for songs of despair and misery this stark photograph takes some beating, the equivalent of pushing self harm videos at vulnerable kids online today (though as there were no actual instructions on the sleeve, I guess RCA had a get out clause). *"Famous Laments to Tug at Your Heart"* ran the strapline on the back. Nobody thought anything of it, except in Australia where they replaced it with a promo photo of Hank instead; loading a six-shooter! The album was a follow up to an earlier RCA release, the equally lighhearted *When Tragedy Struck* (possible heavy airplay number? *There's A Little Box Of Pine On The 7.29*), which had a newspaper on fire for the cover photo. Mind you it wasn't all doom and gloom with Hank, he did break into a smile on some sleeves, and his wardrobe selection on some might just cause you to do the same. We can imagine his amazing coat on the fabulously titled *Hits Covered By Snow* being seen as cutting edge at any fashion show today. Not so much the outfits he and Kelly wore (or in her case just squeezed into) on *Win Some, Lose Some, Lonesome*.

And if you're wondering about Hank's hair here, wonder no more. His son (The Rev. Jimmie Snow) auctioned this off a while ago. *"Hank's wigs are legendary in the music business. Perfect for framing/display..."* according to the sales blurb. We must have missed that on Cash in The Attic.

**Merit Hemmingson • Gästabud**
EMI / Sweden / 1979
*Foto Staffan Anderson. Layout Kerstin Hedenby*

Merit, a female Swedish organist, composer and singer who first made her name popping-up Swedish folk music, has had a remarkable eighty year career across many different musical spheres (including a keep-fit album). So she's excused the occasional bizarre sleeve.
She is the woman on the right with a quartet who all got naked and danced about for the photographer, before the prints were cut out, stuck down and painted over by an artist who did sign this but nobody can decipher it. We count over two dozen pixie things on there and it all ended up looking a proper dog's dinner. Gästabud? An invitation.

# LAUGHS WITH OLAF

**Olaf Sveen • Dance Party**
London Records / Canada / 1973

It's Polka time!
Our Olaf emigrated from his native Norway after the Second World War (one Russia didn't start) and set up with his accordion in Saskatchewan, pumping out a stream of accomplished accordion LPs for London Records (Canada) and the ex-pat Norwegian community.
But it's his routine in front of the camera which Steve picked up on. Olaf seems to have tried to look as bored as possible regardless of what was going on around him. Whether showing off his little leather shorts in the hofbrauhaus or staring out glum-faced on *Dining And Dancing*; while everyone else enjoys themselves, he doesn't. It's the same on *Dance Party*, though if this was the party at its most hedonistic, maybe we'd all feel the same way. Olaf didn't always make the cover; see page 112, where women showing off the hard-landscaping marvels of the Canadian Scandinavian centre makes for one very boring sleeve. And you have to feel sorry for the young girl on *Music For Meditation*, fretting whether the fake fireplace is going to fall on her before the photographer has finished. This sketched sleeve is no better. Let us know if you have spare copies of the last three for Steve's collection.

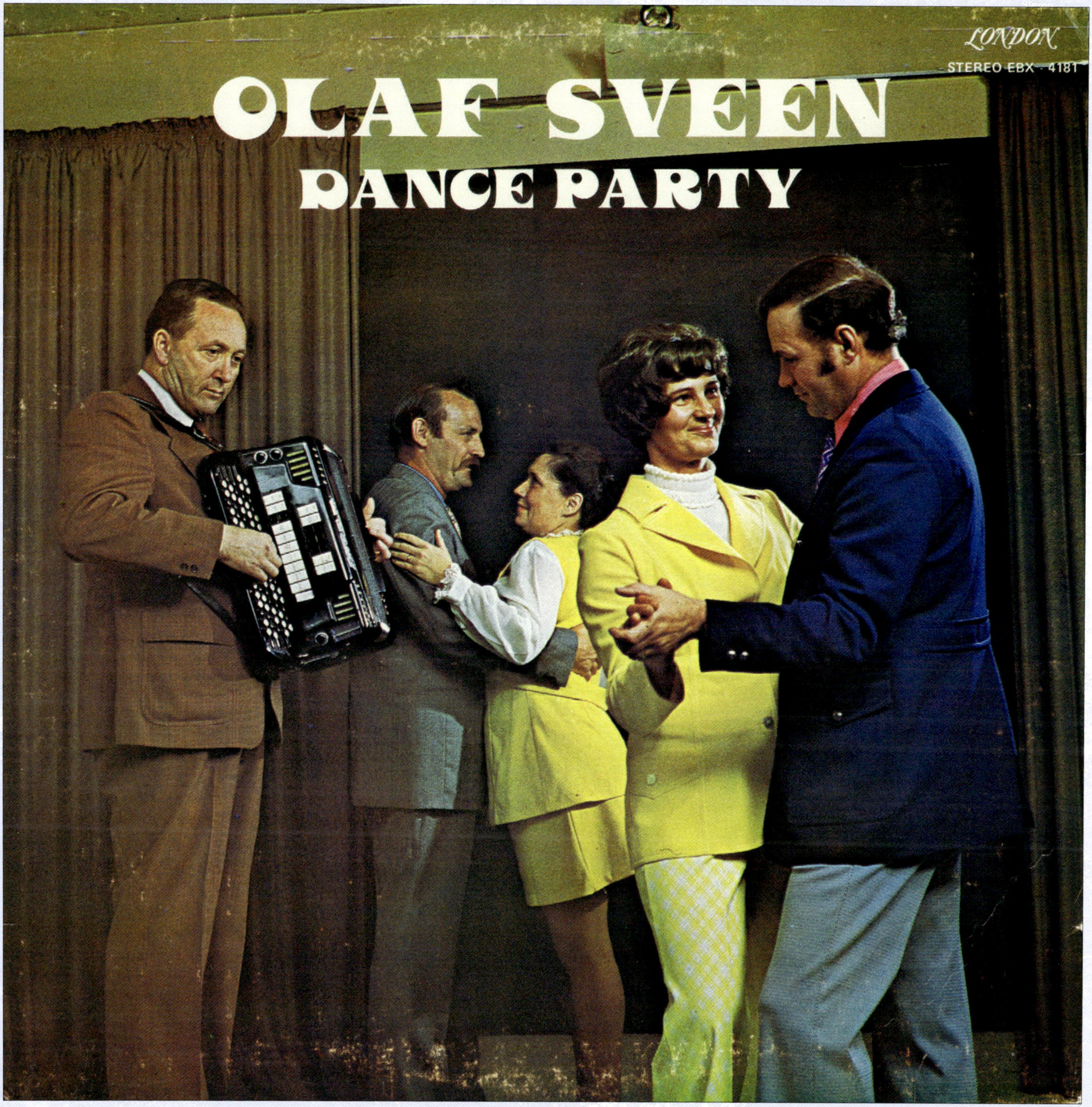
LONDON
STEREO EBX - 4181
OLAF SVEEN
DANCE PARTY

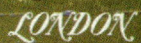

# SHOWBANDS

Clearly you had to be there to understand any of this. But up in Sweden as a musician it seems you were duty bound to call by the fancy dress shop on your way to a photo shoot. **Maltes** opted for bright yellow sleeveless jackets and flared trousers (1975. *Photography and layout Claes-Göran Johansson*), but at least seem to be smirking at the concept. **Bennys** (®) also appear to have 'Gott humor', which you'd kind of need going on stage in those two tone onesies, padded shoulder jackets and stack heeled loafers. They cut an LP a year from 1975 to 1977, then disapppointed bad sleeve collectors by wearing casual suits for their 1984 comeback. **Leif Bloms** cut their first LP in 1973, only disbanding in the mid-1990s after twenty plus albums, many in natty (if at times ill-fitting) jackets like this from 1975. We can only say 'huvudrolls' to the next two covers. *C'mon Let's Twist Again* suggest **Norrasken** on their 1976 debut, though how they managed that in these trousers we're not certain. And yes the cover photo is out of focus; maybe the photographer didn't know where to look either. But then they also thought this was a good logo. Likewise with **Martys**. Amazingly these outfits first appeared on their debut album in 1976 but like Kate Middleton they were not afraid to be seen in the same clobber more than once. And like their musical peers they finally accepted defeat; it was jeans and comfy jumpers for their final album.

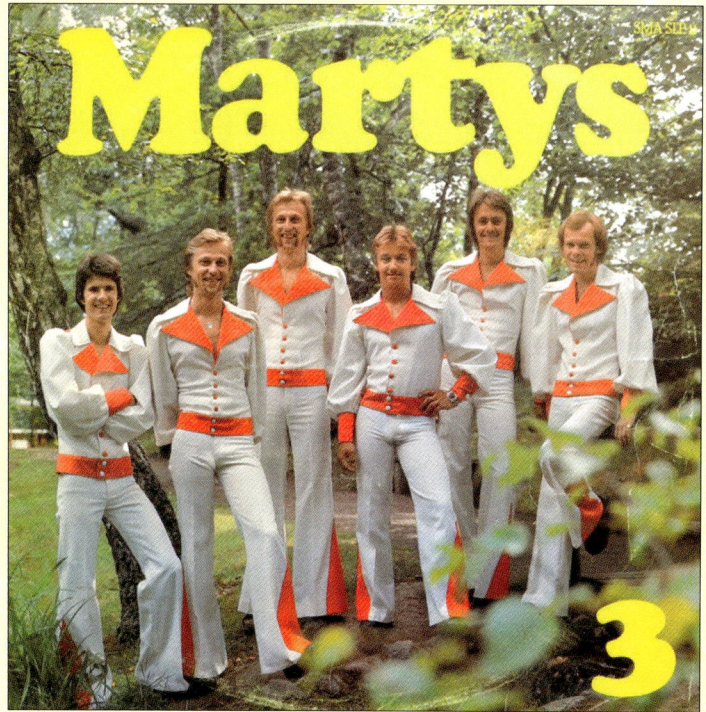

**Treblå & Engul • Mera Blåtiror**
Mallwax / 1976 / Sweden
*Foto Ateljé LE-son. Design Anders F Rönnblom / Studio Sjuttio*

Treblå & Engul, three blues and a yellow (Ulf, Bosse, Fred and Sven). Trebla cut their first album in 1974 as a trio then added Bosse to the line-up for this follow-up of Schlager pop classics. Having posed in branded blue t-shirts first time out (left), they raided Abba's old dressing-up box for this one (opposite page), maybe feeling some of the latter's Eurovision shine would rub off (and hoping the guy at the front would grow in to his suit). What is less clear is why the matching black eyes, unless they argued over who wore the fob watch - round their neck. And as you can see from the previous page, they were one of the better dressed Swedish bands, most of whom come across visually as bad Goodies impressionists. **Gert Jonnys** (left) seem to have run riot with the embroidery attachment on their Husquavana, while the green waistcoats in their promo photo (below) must have been left over from the elves' Christmas grotto. The amazing thing is while Gert Jonnys were doing this, The Clash were releasing *London Calling* and Motorhead had just unleashed *Overkill*. So I think we're allowed to be a little smug at this point. And that's before we explain to them what the slang word 'Gert' means in England.

# ANIMAL FARM

**M. A. Numminen •
M. A. Numminen På
Svenska**
Love Records / Finland /
1972
*Timo Aarniala*

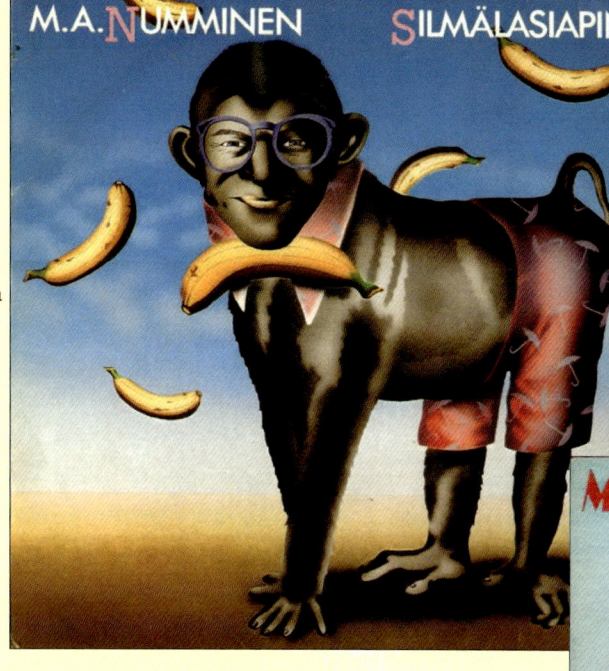

Finnish writer, musician and comedian Mauri Antero Numminen (who looks like a sort of Scandinavian Captain Beefheart) has crossed many musical genres over his long 36 album career, from pioneering electronic music to children's songs. Many of them appeared on Love Records, who used illustrator Timo Aarniala for quite a few of the covers. Let's just say the curious quirky style would not have given Alan Aldridge any sleepless nights!
As well as froggie, Numminen seems to have gone for the half man half beast look on a number of his albums, including here as a camel and a monkey. He also did this equally strange looking album in English (*"restrained solo song from Nordic soil"*) on the right, which I must have missed in our local record shop's new release rack.

# LIKE A SHIP ON THE OCEAN

**Kjell Kraghe Och Ricke Löw's Orkester • Vind I Seglen**
Koster Records Sweden 1981
*Main foto Carlaforlaget. Foto of Kjell Kraghee Kjells Foto AB*

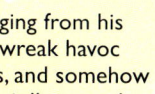

Swedish entertainer Kjell seems airly obsessed with boats and sailing judging from his discography, and here rises from the ocean like the legendary Kraken to wreak havoc on local shipping, all beaming smiles, blonde hair and oversized spectacles, and somehow taking the snap himself according to the sleeve credits. When not singing jolly songs he busied himself writing revues for his local theatre. Those long winter nights.... Mind you, here are the mighty **Groundhogs** doing the same thing in Epping Forest back in 1968.

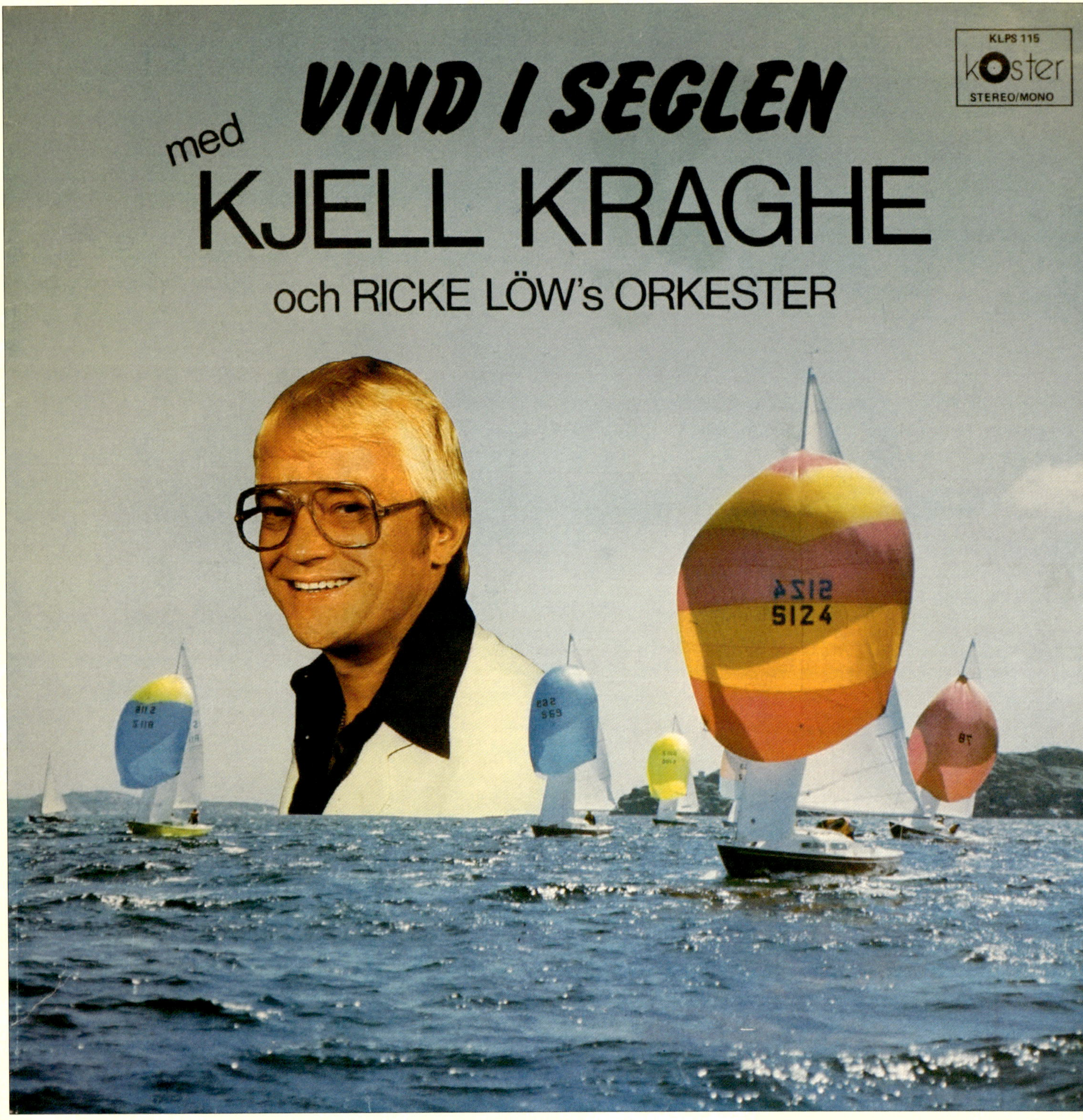
KLPS 115
koster
STEREO/MONO
VIND I SEGLEN
med
KJELL KRAGHE
och RICKE LÖW's ORKESTER
5124

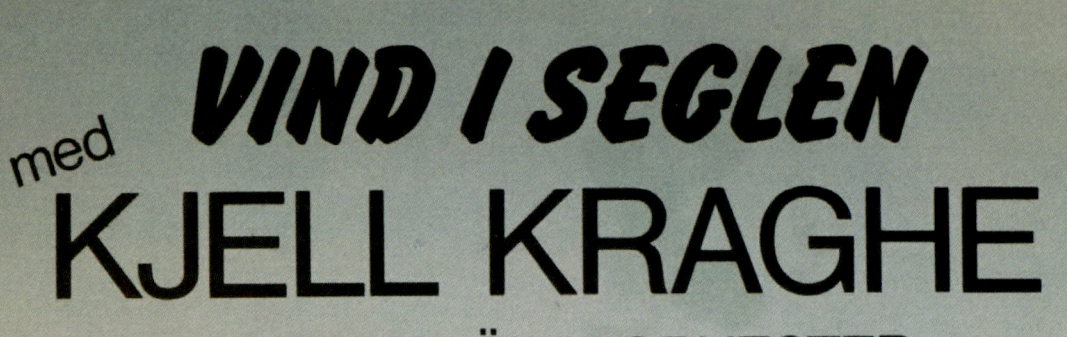

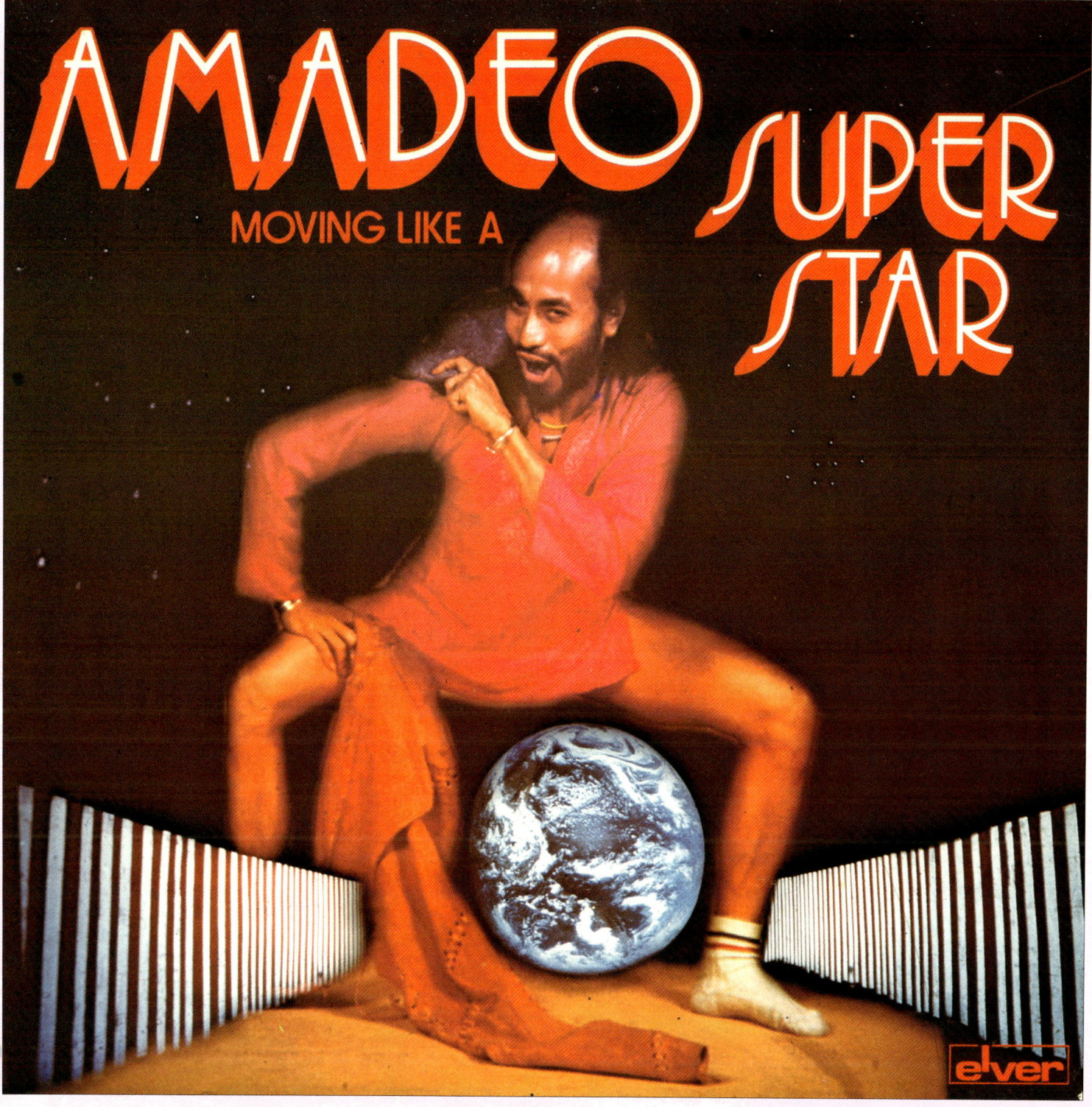

# BIZARRE DISCO DUCKS

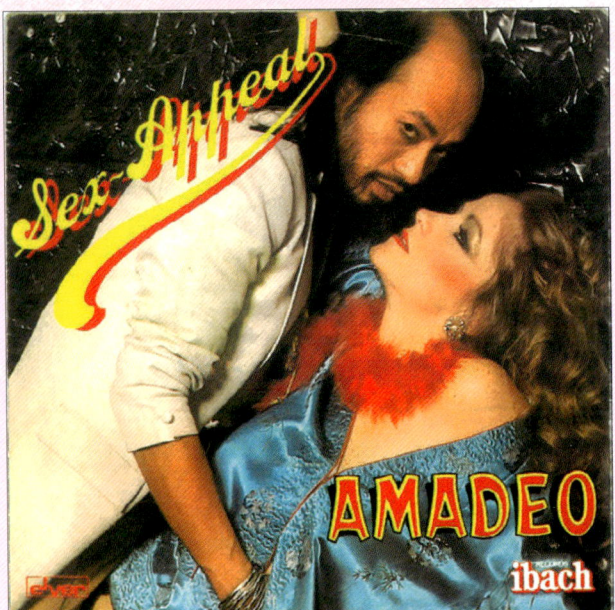

### Amadeo • Moving Like A Super Star
Elver Records / Belgium / 1977
*Photo Dao / Paris*

Does a superstar really excrete planet shaped movements? And if so, why do they think we need to see it?! Riding the disco boom, this was Amadeo's album debut and several European countries thought better of it, redesigning the cover (or relegated the shot to the back) to avoid this unfortunate image. Amadéo Barrios cut records into the late 1980s (see left) but has since returned to choreography, dance and, perhaps fittingly, meditation.

### Village People • Renaissance
RCA Victor / USA / 1981
*Art direction, design Phyllis Chotin, Michele Hart. Photography J Steven Arnold*

After several years at the top of the disco era dressed in their trademark fancy-dress key worker outfits (as on the single cover below), Village People were reinvented as a New Romantic outfit for their seventh album (right). Even amongst the excesses of this musical era, *Renaissance* just ends up looking naff. The four guys in the alternate police line-up maybe, but having the two 'important' members of the group awkwardly looming over it all just upsets the karma. Musically the reviews were not kind either and they were soon back in builders' onesies and cowboy hats for the follow up.

### Ziggie Addy • Touch Me
Hansa International / 1976 / Germany

It is not the only appearance of the Hansa label in the book, but it is the first time for cruelty to squirrels. Ziggie - real name Ziggienorllar Addy - had a bit of a hit with this disco cut, which was released all across Europe. The follow up wasn't, so this became a certified one-hit wonder, relegated to *20 Super Disco Busters* for the last few sales. We're not sure what happened to Ziggie after that.
Or indeed the squirrel.

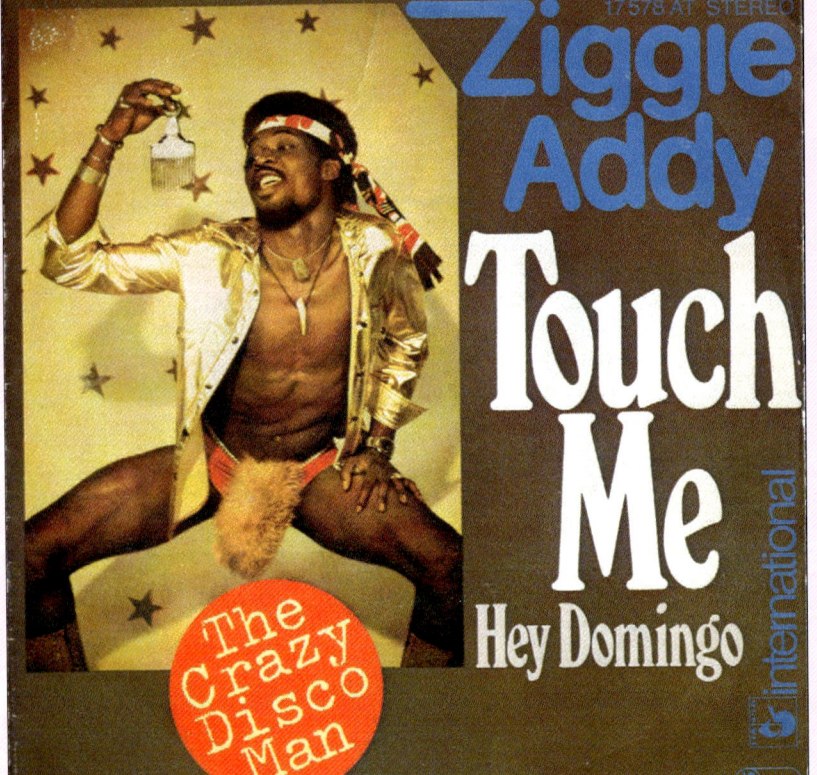

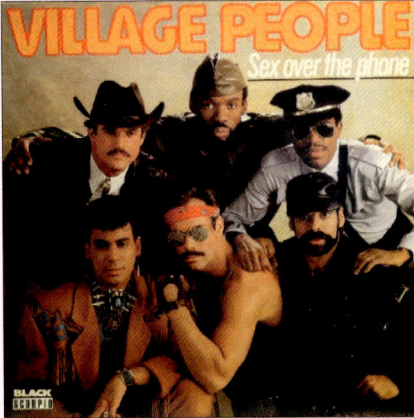

# THE EYES HAVE IT

**Queen • The Miracle**
Parlophone / UK / 1989
*Richard Baker Artwork Quantel Graphic Paintbox Operator. Richard Gray Design. Simon Fowler Photography*

This cover still seems to divide a lot of fans. So well known you tend to pass the LP by in charity shops (and it is turning up there quite a lot now), but once you take a studied look, it is quietly disturbing. Then you turn it over and it gets *very* disturbing! I always felt Queen sleeves were overblown (art college boy Freddie was wise to stick with the day job) and effects like this are more in keeping with a horror film poster.
Initially four very good portraits were taken (Simon Fowler was the go-to guy for musicians at the time), printed out and torn roughly to get them to overlap. From there they were put into an image manipulation system, the Quantel Graphic Paintbox (used for TV and film work) to blend all the faces together (above left). Photoshop had *just* been launched but wasn't up to this level of work yet. And the 2005 parody above by Gerson is equally off-putting!

# DISCO DUCKS

**Jumbo • City Girls**
Pye International / UK (Hansa International / Germany) 1977
*Art Direction and concept Manfred Vormstein. Illustration Jürgen F Rogner.*

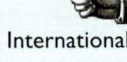

German disco band Jumbo cut a swathe through the clubs in the country during the late Seventies on the back of their hit debut single and album *Sexy Lady*. *City Girls* was the follow up album; out went the naked woman reclining on the beach which decorated the first, and in came a mystic flying black guy soaring above a crashed airliner, bookended with a couple of poorly painted scantily-clad women. Vormstein claimed the idea, and as he did several hundred very different sleeves for Ariola and other German labels, we assume he had something in mind when commissioning this, but what it was we're still trying to puzzle out.

Tellingly the Japanese would have nothing to do with it and got Rogner (his striking snake / bird / woman adorning Amanda Lear's album *Never Trust A Pretty Face* below will be remembered by some) to do a completely different illustration (above); you don't need to be a student of overt racism to figure out why.

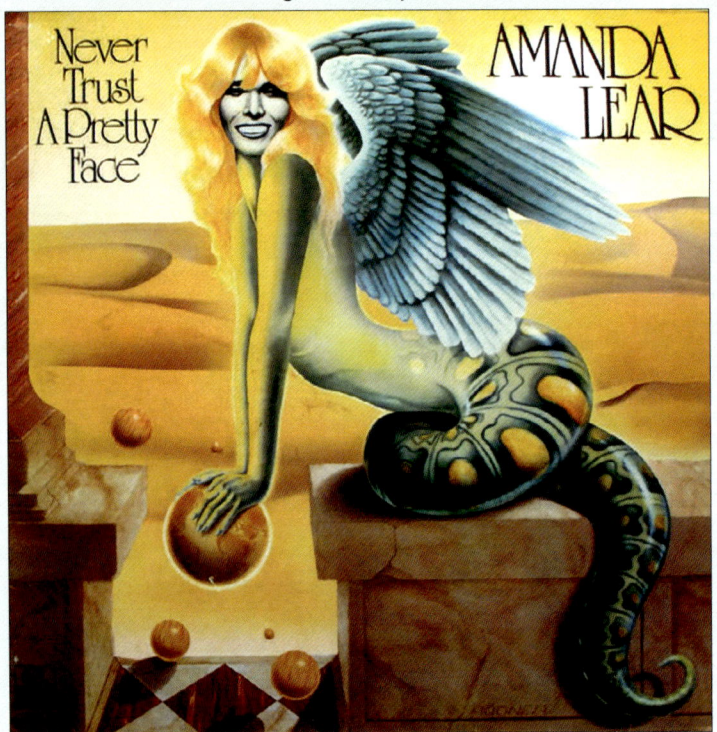

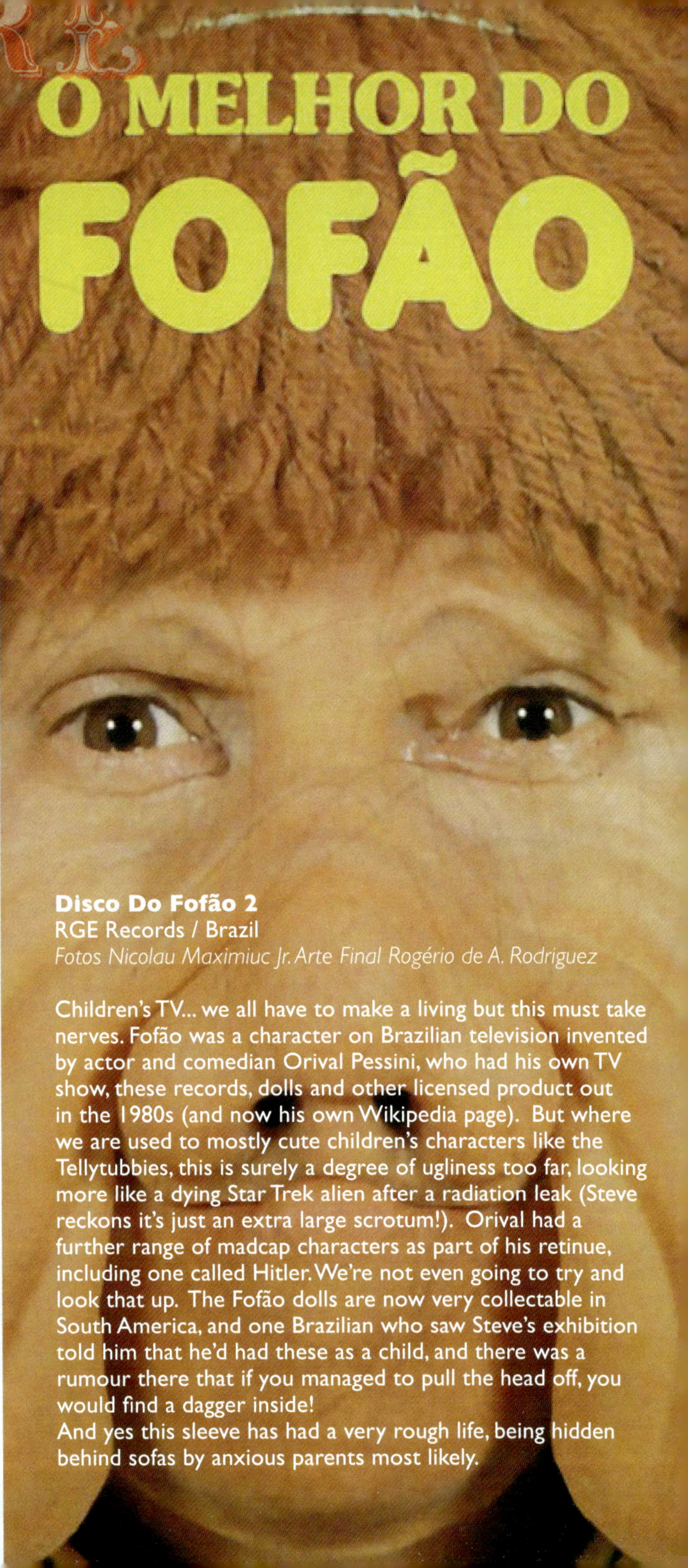

# O MELHOR DO FOFÃO

**Disco Do Fofão 2**
RGE Records / Brazil
*Fotos Nicolau Maximiuc Jr. Arte Final Rogério de A. Rodriguez*

Children's TV... we all have to make a living but this must take nerves. Fofão was a character on Brazilian television invented by actor and comedian Orival Pessini, who had his own TV show, these records, dolls and other licensed product out in the 1980s (and now his own Wikipedia page). But where we are used to mostly cute children's characters like the Tellytubbies, this is surely a degree of ugliness too far, looking more like a dying Star Trek alien after a radiation leak (Steve reckons it's just an extra large scrotum!). Orival had a further range of madcap characters as part of his retinue, including one called Hitler. We're not even going to try and look that up. The Fofão dolls are now very collectable in South America, and one Brazilian who saw Steve's exhibition told him that he'd had these as a child, and there was a rumour there that if you managed to pull the head off, you would find a dagger inside!

And yes this sleeve has had a very rough life, being hidden behind sofas by anxious parents most likely.

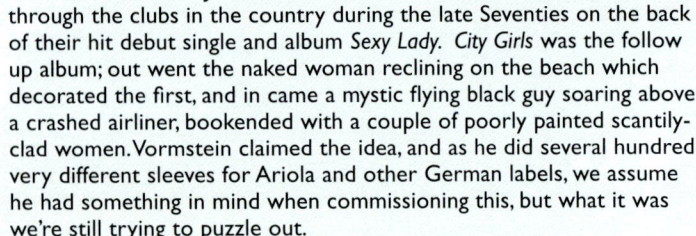

# METAL MISTAKES

### Deep Purple • Shades Of
EMI Harvest Heritage / UK / 1987

Deep Purple's sleeves won a number of industry and press awards in the Seventies, and it was only after the band split in 1976 that things began to drift. And then this washed up in shops. EMI were keen to repromote their progressive label Harvest via a Harvest Heritage series in 1977, all in new covers. Except whoever they put in charge hadn't got a clue and signed off this awful new sleeve for Deep Purple's 1968 debut (never mind the admittedly dated looking original (right) had never been on Harvest!). Happily the band's manager saw proofs and vetoed it, so EMI came up with something else. The reissue sold modestly over ten years but eventually needed a repress, which is when somebody at EMI pulled the rejected cover art out by mistake. When I got in touch to ask if dead babies arms really was what a Deep

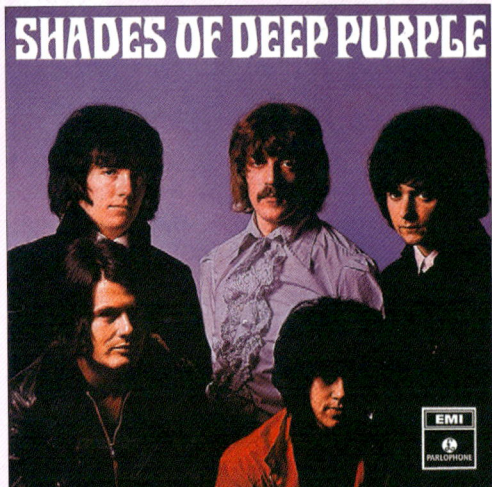

Purple cover should look like, EMI realised the error, and reprinted the correct sleeve. Needless to say copies of the withdrawn edition which had been sold have now become a real rarity and fetch up to £200 on a good day.

### Black Sabbath • Born Again
Vertigo / UK / 1983
*Design Steve Joule*

This cheap looking cover is a one off from Ian Gillan's short spell fronting his former rock rivals (Osbourne and Iommi having fallen out with each other). Joule said later he didn't really want the job, so quickly photocopied a baby photo from a part-weekly encyclopedia, stuck some horns on, coloured it red, and was very surprised when Vertigo got back to say Iommi liked it. It was then too late to do anything better! Others in the band were less kind and drummer Bill Ward quickly disowned it: *"I didn't have any participation in the album cover. When I saw it, I hated it."*
Ian Gillan famously told one journalist that he vomited when he first saw the picture. Kerrang! put it at No. 2 on their readers list of "10 Worst Album Sleeves in Metal/Hard Rock". The NME included it on a list of the "Sickest album covers ever", while his old manager once told Osbourne that his children resembled the one on the cover!

# VOX CANTORIS

**Kris Jensen Sings • Torture**
Hickory Records / USA / 1962

Printed and manufactured by the Modern Album Corporation, Kris says on the back *"Thanks to all the DeeJays who played my record of Torture and made this possible"*. Clearly he had never read the words out loud. But while clean-cut Kris might be someone you would let your daughter date, once you see the word *Torture* in big large horror-film style letters above a photograph, alarm bells might tend to go off big-time. For good measure the title is then painted serial killer style on the back, while the previous owner of this copy has begun to colour bits in blood red for some reason. It's no surprise this was his only album, singles were the main pop medium and Kris issued two dozen of them over a ten year period, though *Torture* (originally written for The Everley Brothers though Kris beat them to it) was his only hit.

**Anton Disselkoen • Why Do I Sing?...**
*Art direction Mike Burnette. Photo Jack Bunting*

Another undated self-released Christian 'pop' album. Calling your album *Why Do I Sing?* was clearly asking for trouble, with the title track as the opening medley (interpolating *"His Eye Is On The Sparrow"*). As someone at Steve's exhibition said *"The guy really does look he is in the middle of an existential crisis, 'yes, why DO I sing?'"* The cover is technically woeful too with a lack of tonal range which would drive any old school reprographic technician barmy. The back cover photo would have made a far better sleeve. If only the Lord had sent him a sign about this.

**Foster Brooks • "Sings"**
The Good Music Record Co. / USA / 1982
*Design Eileen Dovidauskas. Photography By Bill Drummond*

Placing the word *"Sings"* in speech marks here begs all sorts of questions! We also like the attempt to big this up with K-Tel style '20 Great Hits', and 'as seen on TV', though where is never mentioned. And just what is a 'double length recording' anyway?

### Jim Post • I Love My Life
Mountain Railroad Records / USA / 1978
*Graphic design Christine Usinger / Cover photography Jo Dose*

"Cheer up mate, it might never happen..." But clearly it already has. If you're going to call your album *I Love My Life*, why look so darn miserable on the front? Jim had a Billboard Top 10 chart hit in the late Sixties but despite recording for the next 30 years never repeated the success, so maybe he had something to be mournful about. Perhaps Jim was bemoaning the album coming out just as punk and new wave were getting into their stride. He did later get onto the Ellen DeGeneres Show in a slot called "Awesome Album Covers", but sadly this was an ironic feature. Still, could have been worse, see the inner sleeve, where he is attempting to get towed along by butterflies, and the moon howls at *him*.

### Taco • Under My Tight Skin
RCA / Germany / 1984 12" single
*Fotografie Und Design Stefan Bohle Studio Icks*

Dutch singer Taco Ockerse followed the fashions over his lengthy career on vinyl, kicking off all moody, veering to full white make up for a bit of synth-pop (above right) and then this rather spooky photo montage, which looks like an out-take from some dystopian sci-fi cyborg movie. You could almost date this from the typography and graphic design alone. Not a hit, Taco switched to sub-George Michael photo-shoots with jacket sleeves rolled up before moving into acting. 28 years later Keyshia Cole's cover designer comes up with the exact same idea (below) and it still looks spooky!

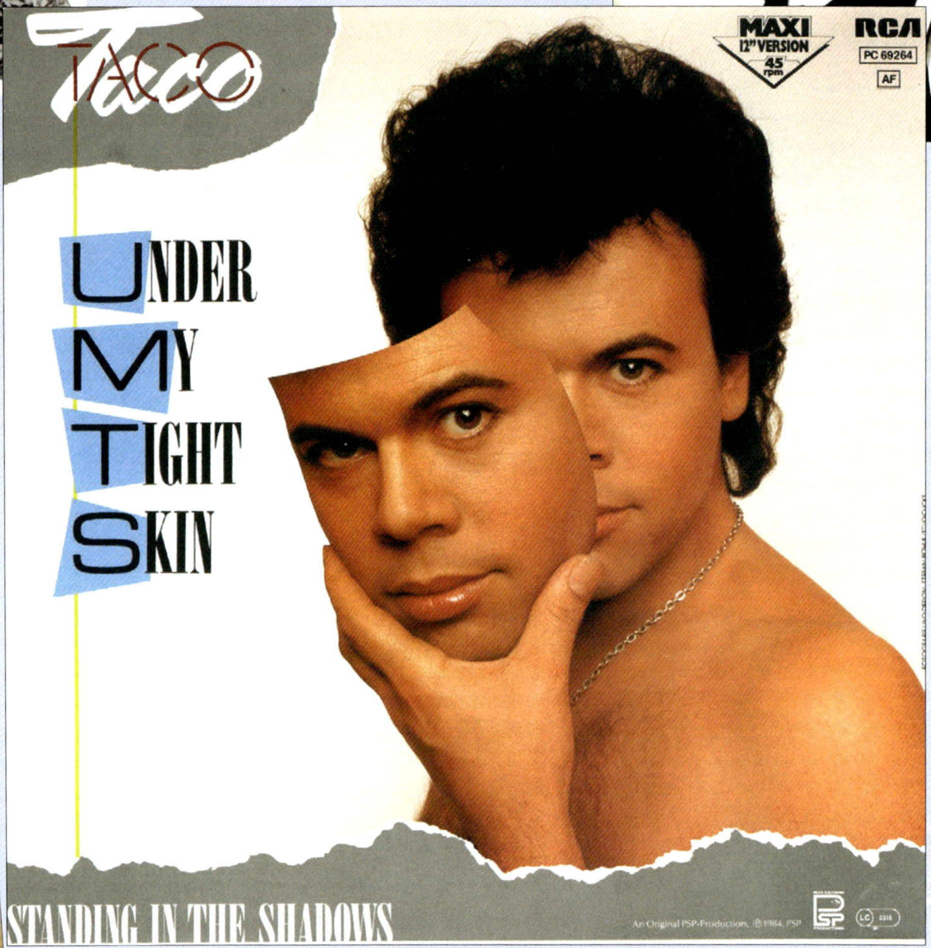

130

# JAZZERCISE

C'mon, surely it should have been called *Gym & Tonic,* ladies? Or *Yodelling In The Alps With Veronique And Davina.* The celebrity exercise album is a market which the internet has now largely killed off. Famous people trying to look as if they spend their lives in the gym, when in reality they are keeping up an inane grin in Sheila Rock's photo studio for a couple of hours before zipping off to bank the cheque.

Back in the early Eighties you were nobody without a tie-in fitness record, and a FREE booklet of how to do it photographs.

Although such is the speed of celebrity burn out, today you usually need to do a web-search to find out who some of them are. Over to New Zealand for **Carol O'Halloran • Jazzercise** (left, 1981). Here the photo budget looks as stretched as the badly fitting outfit, with Carol doing her best jazz hands look as well as a worrying haka impression (though we're not sure why her arms fade in and out). The album went gold and was top of the NZ charts for six weeks - above the Rolling Stones! Carol continues to promote well-being to this day.

From the USA in 1982 (top left) for country music lovers, on the very dubiously named Plantation Records label, **How The Waist Was Won** (*"The country way from True Grit to True Fit"*) wins out for worst punning title in our book, plus a terrifying combination of lycra swim suits and combinations. Not to mention mad hats and white cowboy boots (but mercifully no sign of John Wayne).

We assume that is June LaSalvia on the front but frustratingly there is no sign anywhere of her wonderfully named back up musicians, The Lean Jeans Band.

At least **Shape Up & Dance With Felicity Kendal** (1981) features a national treasure. Several more celebs joined in this series, including George Best, looking a bit of a berk with his arms around Mary 'Caddyshack 2' Stavin. For some reason the blokes look even more idiotic on these records, check the **Lionel Blair** album left (**Aerobic Dancing** / Conifer Records / 1983), though try and avoid glimpsing *those* shorts. Still, maybe there was something in this one, as Lionel sired three kids, was still tap dancing in his late Eighties and made it to the grand age of 92.
**Max Greger** was a German jazz musician, saxophonist, band leader and conductor who saw an opening (and sales opportunity) in the keep-fit market between his regular Tanz pop albums. **Trimm Und Tanz Dich Fit** (1973 top right) looks so relentlessly Germanic. Full marks to all for ditching the lycra, but we're not sure how much stretching you could manage in those trousers (or what the Damp 2000 sticker was about). Lastly comes the fabulous **Slenderide** from America. It looks like the cover model (hair specially done for the work-out) is being brought back through The Time Tunnel, so realistically she could have been anywhere, anytime (the disc is undated). With the model struggling on the left of the cover to keep her balance, this was produced to tie-in with the budget exercise bicycle shown; Peloton for the analogue generation (though Slenderide never had to issue a product recall!).

**V/A • Prince Jammy Presents Vol 3**
World Enterprise Records / USA
*Graphics by Tony Nero*

Leonardo da Vinci expressed the essence of perspective as *"to make what is flat appear in relief"*. Developed in the 15th century by Renaissance artists, it appears not to have reached fifth grade art classes in junior high, where this pencil masterpiece might have struggled to get half marks. There were four of these compilations, put together by Reggae producer Lloyd James (Prince Jammy). The first two were quite eye catching (with a cut out photo of a boxer's arm), after which this naïve drawing turned up. And while the designs have a bit of a Sixties' Jamaican dub vibe about them, they actually came out in the Eighties. The illustrator has hundreds of covers under his belt, a number of which exhibit a similarly confused approach to imagery and design (as seen on the other two examples), and some depicting overtly graphic depictions of the sexist lyrics we can't show here.

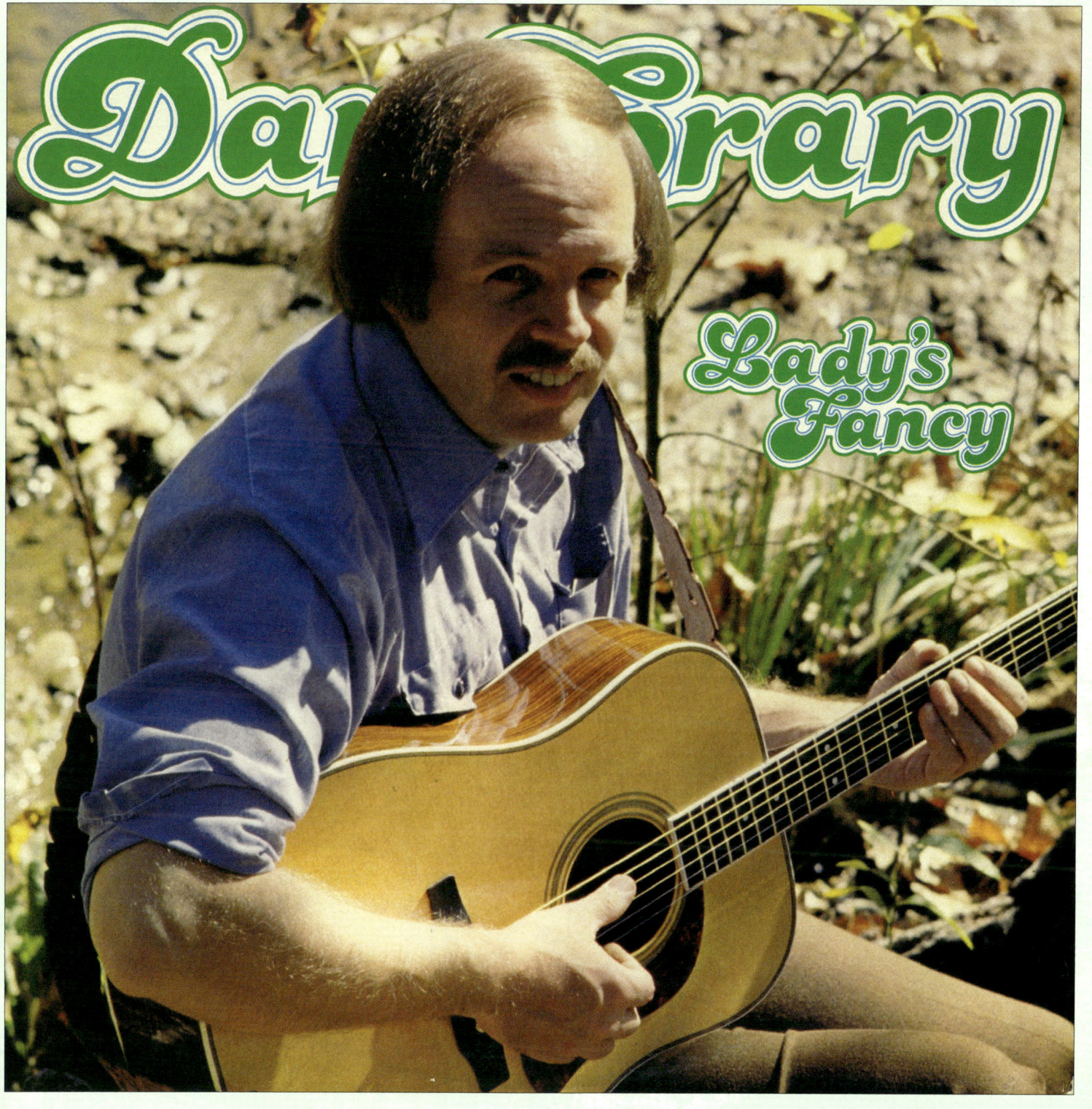

### Dan Crary • Lady's Fancy
Rounder Records / USA / 1977
*Art direction and Cover design Ron Johnson. Photo Jeff Smith*

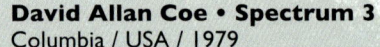

"One of the things you should never do is write the liner notes for your own album…" Says noted bluegrass guitarist Dan, quoted on the back of this album. Another thing you should not do is cover up your name on the front sleeve with the photo. Or style your hair-do after Max Wall. Lady's fancy? Let's not take a vote. Happily, whoever sorted the cover for his follow up (*Sweet Southern Girl*) did a much better job, aided by a decent photographer and not relying on the mid-day sun for lighting.

### Ruth McKenny • I'm So Hot And I Need You
Fleet / Netherlands / 1979 7" single

Well, nothing like a bit of plain speaking. And the next time someone asks you to name a famous Belgian, his real name is Rudy Van Laer.
Bassist / singer Ruth was later (inset) trying to keep control of *That Tiger In My Body*. Having managed this clearly difficult task he went on to have any number of hits in Benelux, indeed is still out there, dad rocking for all he is worth.

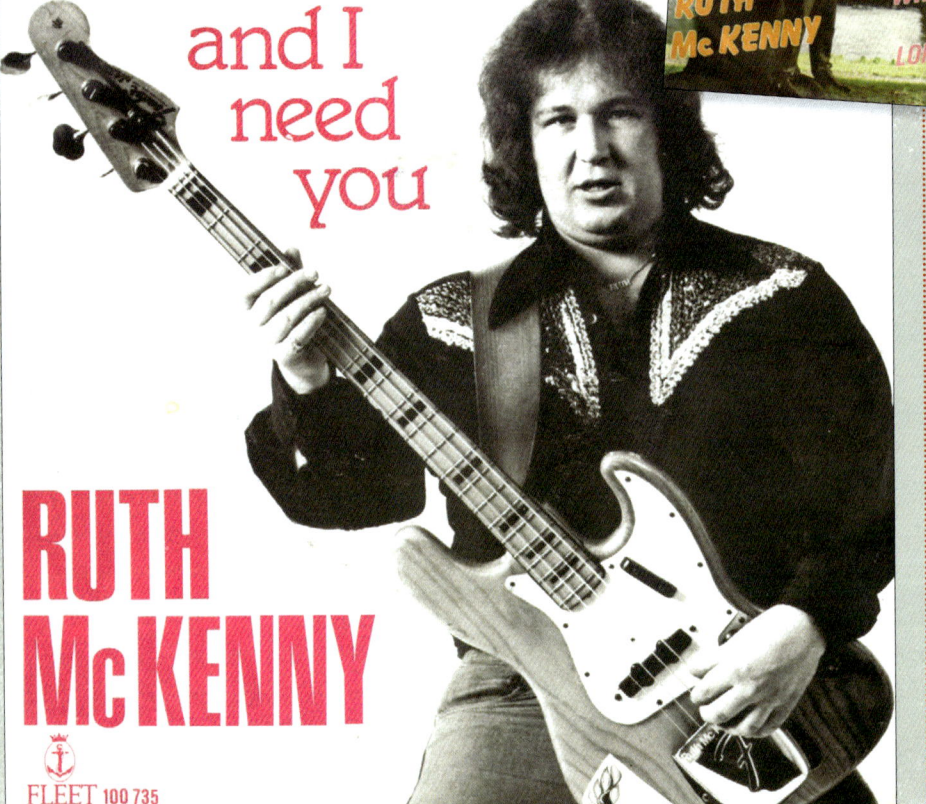

### David Allan Coe • Spectrum 3
Columbia / USA / 1979
*Front Brian Hagiwara, back David Allan Coe*

I'm surprised the Donald didn't hire him to open his rallies…
Coe's life must be worth a decent biographer's time; coming to music having spent time in a penitentiary learning songwriting from Screamin' Jay Hawkins and living in a hearse when he got out.
This kind of starts to explain the 'don't mess with me' look on the sleeve. Coe kicked off with 1969's *Penitentiary Blues* LP then here unleashed the outlaw country concept album on the world. *"Perhaps now my luck will change,"* he adds on the notes. Technically the sleeve photographs are top notch, as they should be given Hagiwara's long career as a cover photographer, but Coe makes it all looks very end of the pier theatrical (and just a little Homer Simpson) today. The LP followed 1977's lovely *Texas Moon*, below, on which the band bared their posteriors across the front cover (except in Spain where they substituted a picture of Coe and the moon!). Vintage police mug shots of Coe decorated the back sleeve.

### Žarko Dančuo • Žana / Ne Ljubi Me Nikad Više
Jugoton / Yugoslavia / 1978 7" single
*Design I. Ivezić.  Ž. Milutinović*

Žarko paid his dues in local prog outfit Roboti in the Sixties (*Hold On, I'm Coming...* was track 2 on their debut EP, which would probably not have made the Radio 1 playlist at the time). He then went solo, covering Western hits, before following his father into pop cabaret.  Clearly unable to get to Seditionaries for his clobber, this smart / casual outfit had to serve.  It's just that normally to try and impress the girls you stuff a pair of socks down the front, rather than grab a handful...  He retired in 2005. Hurt.

### Prince • Lovesexy
Paisley Park / USA / 1988
*Cover Photo, Photography By Jean Baptiste Mondino. Design Laura LiPuma Nash*

Despite his musical status, quite a few of Prince's covers are fairly ropey or look like they were done at speed. Fans enjoy lively forum discussions as to the worst (one commenting that the *Emancipation* LP cover looked like a bad Scientology brochure!).
Never exactly a shrinking violet, Mr. Nelson went full billy bollocks for his tenth album, to reinforce the lyrical themes of '*positivity, self-improvement, spirituality and God*'.  Not all stores were convinced; some refused to stock it or over-wrapped the album.
Best known for his fashion photography, Jean Baptiste Mondino did hundreds of record sleeves for French and international acts and technically the shot is flawless.  Sometimes known as "the flower penis" sleeve today, it quickly made it into Rolling Stone's Twenty Dirtiest Covers Of All Time poll in 2019.  In some far east countries they got over their issues by printing Prince up some little blue trousers, as per this pirate cassette edition (right).
For my money, the German single *Sexuality* is one of the worst looking Prince covers, though as it was a German only release it is doubtful if the man had much say over this; it was probably done in half an hour in the design department at Warner Bros. It'll set you back over £100 today.

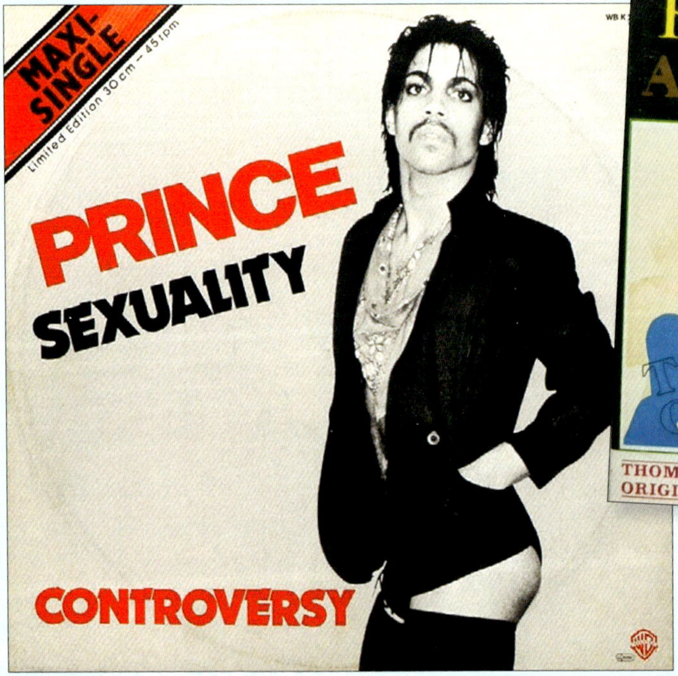

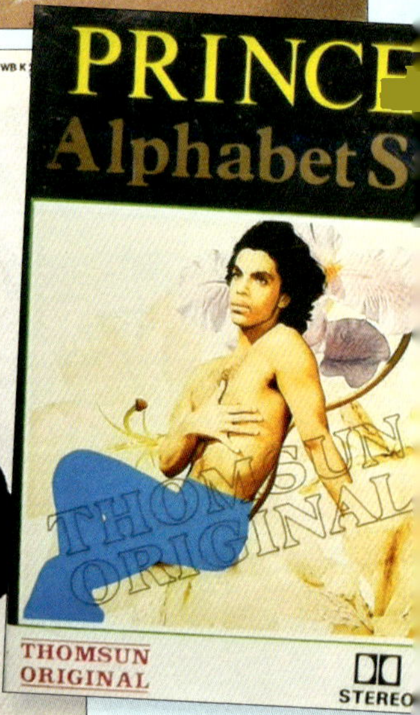

# BIZARRE

**Mato Grosso • Mato Grosso**
Ariola / Brazil / 1982
*Capa e Fotos Luiz Fernandos Borges da Fonseca. Coordenaçào Gràfica J C Melio*

Many have admired Millais' painting *Ophelia* at the Tate, but Mato Grosso (real name Ney de Sousa Pereira) seems to have decided to recreate it for himself in a river in Brazil (Mato Grosso being a state in that country). Just watch out for those piranhas. It's quite a strange and indeed ambitious image (you could imagine Peter Gabriel going for the concept) with a fold-out poster inside as well. Shorn of any context though it just looks very bonkers forty years on. That context is that Ney was pushing at the boundaries, bravely presenting himself as an *"androgynous, gender-bending performer"* (according to Beyond Carnival: Male Homosexuality in Twentieth Century Brazil). Quite how gazing at the camera while an eagle plonks itself on your head (on this later cover, right) is less clear. Album sleeves in Brazil were often printed on really cheap thin card, which is why they often suffer so badly from wear and tear (as here).

**Sim • Quoi Ma Gueule**
Trema / France / 1981 7" single
*Artwork C. Laplace. Photography M. Dreyfuss*

In complete contrast...Winning first prize in a 1939 funny face competition aged just 13 set Sim (aka Simon Jacques Eugène Berryer) on the path to showbiz. He cut his first record in 1957 and bowed out with this single (left) in 1981, though he carried on acting until less than a year before he died. Seemingly the record (and cover) is a bit of a dig at French chanson legend Johnny Halliday, who I would have thought was perfect capable of doing that himself in later years. Hence the leathers, though the balding crown is Sim's own rather than clever make-up. For clever make-up you need to see his 1976 album cover. So here it is.

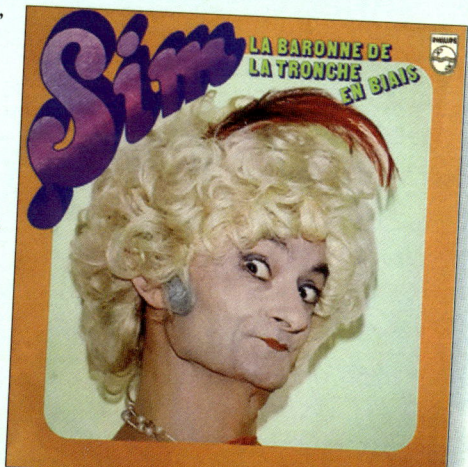

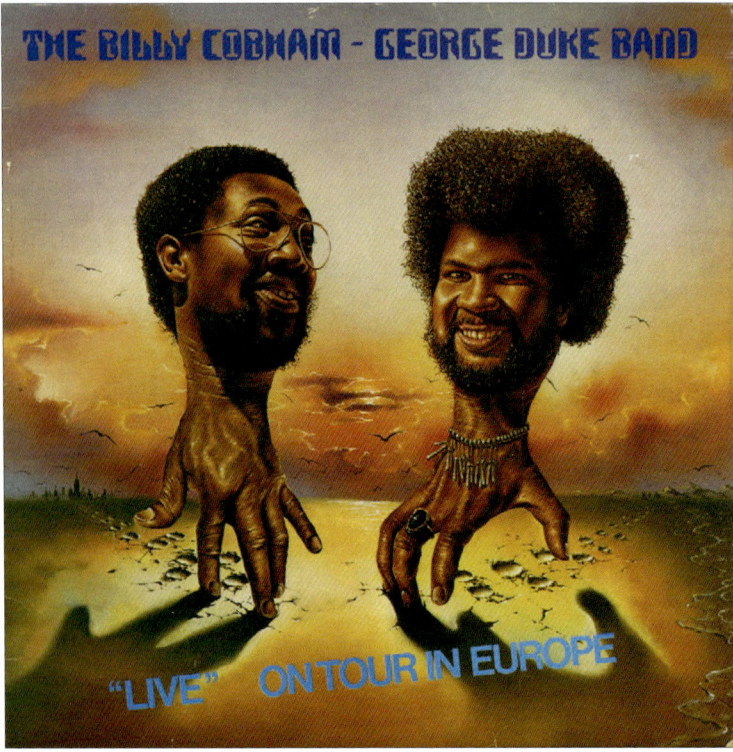

# FACE OFF

**George Jones • I Wanta Sing**
CBS / USA / 1977
*Bus illustration Gene Wilkes. Album design Bill Barnes*

The endless road is a bit of an sleeve cliché, but old George (an award-winning country music singer responsible for numerous hit records, and married to Tammy Wynette for a time) here looks like he's been taking something hefty to keep himself awake at the wheel during the long lonesome night. If the hooter next to his ear didn't do the trick. George was a bit of a drinker at one time, and one of his wives hid the car keys when she was out so he couldn't make it to the off-licence eight miles away. But she forgot the keys to the ride-on mower. *"It might have taken an hour and a half or more for me to get to the liquor store, but get there I did!"* he recounted in his autobiography.
Airbrush artist Gene Wilkes only did a handful of sleeves which mostly show his interest in 60s' counter culture imagery, all better than this! On the back here, there is a cut-out and make model of a tour bus, like you used to get on the back of cornflakes boxes, but no sign of a little George to stick on the front.

**The Billy Cobham George Duke Band • Live On Tour In Europe**
Atlantic Records / UK / 1976
*Cover illustration Jim Warren. Design Cal Schenkel*

Another in the 'ideas which ought not to have been put down on a canvas' category (top left). It's well executed and you sort of understand how it made the suggestion box (although only one of the pair was a keyboard player), but it does end up being very much on the eerie science fiction pulp novel end of the spectrum, jovial faces aside. Designer Cal Schenkel is known to most album sleeve connoisseurs for his brilliant work with Frank Zappa, and knew how to pick a good illustrator, but this could give you sleepless nights.

**Cleveland Eaton • Half And Half**
Gamble Records / USA / 1973
*Design Ed Lee. Cover illustration Ignacio Gomez*

Cleveland Josephus Eaton II (really) was an American jazz double bassist, producer, arranger, composer, publisher and head of his own record company. But not a Taurus. He went solo with this LP on his own label, doing a minimalist design himself. Signed by Gamble a year later, the LP was repackaged (left), with Cleveland portrayed as a jolly looking bull. Cleveland (who later got a two week gig with Count Basie which lasted 17 years) also deserves a mention for the title of the follow up LP, *Plenty Good Eaton*, a jazz-funk classic despite the Les Dawson entry level pun!

# FACE OFF

**Tim Hart • Tim Hart**
Chrysalis / UK / 1979
*Sleeve by Adrian Chesterman*

The illustrator here has an impressive portfolio across all types of media as well as record sleeves; the Motorhead *Bomber* cover is one of his for goodness sake. But Tim Hart, one of the founders of Steeleye Span, has ended up looking like he already regrets the cover of this, his one and only solo album (mind you Steeleye Span were not exactly blessed cover wise for most of their career). It's like all the elements are present but somehow mis-matched.

The contrast between this and Todd (opposite) could not be greater, and the budget for this must have been many times more too, but it still presses the slightly queasy button for us. Notice the strange tree trunks in the landscape too... and the melting fingers!

**Todd •
With Love From Me To You**
private pressing  *Cover design Gerald Hahn*

This one always draws gasps when first sighted at Steve's exhibition. First issued in 1979 (some researchers suggest it may be a little older), collectors prices soared to above the £400 mark in recent years, prompting a 500 run vinyl reissue from Todd himself in 2013, in black or clear vinyl, with a handful including a handwritten note from the man inside. Indeed this run was close to being sold out when we looked into it, though downloads will one assumes be available for all eternity. The original cover image was printed onto paper sheets, which Todd stuck to blank sleeves, and this reissue looses a little of that vintage d.i.y feel, but the cover illustration remains as mesmeric as ever. And full marks to Todd for not correcting the original wonky rub-down lettering either!
Just so you know, the Acid Archives site suggests of the album's material: *"It's dorky, but sincere and endearing nonetheless. Outsider music at it's finest."*

# FACE OFF

### 31 Knots • Trump Harm
Polyvinyl Records / USA / 2011
*Design, Artwork By Jay Winebrenner*

Proof that despite the astonishing developments in digital image manipulation in the last 25 years, you can still produce some very grotty results if you do not learn the software basics. Otherwise it ends up looking like you snipped round colour prints from Happy Snaps and stuck them onto a sunset taken on your last holiday in Spain. Unless…
The cover found itself onto 'worst sleeve' lists double quick. It's a shame, as the band's other covers are often really interesting design wise.

### Manal • Manal
Mandioca / Argentina / 1972 reissue

It's easy to smirk at media jobs such as 'image consultant', but here's a band who would have been well advised to bring one along on this photo shoot. Their 1970 debut album was issued on one of their friends' labels as, despite their popularity on the Argentine blues rock scene, nobody would give them a deal. RCA finally signed them for a second LP and also reissued the first in this grim new sleeve.
You can see the kind of Cream power trio look the (uncredited) photographer was after, but apart from breaking the golden rule of making sure studio lights do not reflect in people's glasses (it's golden rule number two, after 'take the lens cap off') you also need to make sure your other two subjects don't seem so damn scary (the bloke on the right looks like he's taken his own eye-lids off).

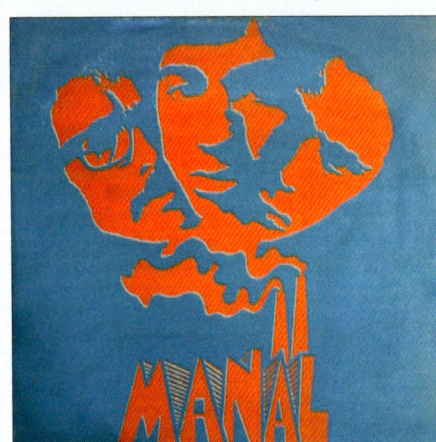

The photo is an out-take from their second album cover shoot which mostly made them look fairly human, so there must have been better shots. (I really like the 1970 Uruguayan version here, with the off register agit-prop vibe, but it is now a £250 record so I'll pass!)

### Horch • Der Lautenschläger
Amiga / GDR / 1986
*Fotos Jürgen Domes. Gestaltung Mo Prust*

Fours guys don fancy dress and try to win the lady's favor by showing off on the violin, recorder and goodness knows what. Even assuming she's not tied to the chair and could escape, she looks far from enthralled. Horch began in East Germany in 1979 playing folk-rock on medieval instruments, synthesisers and crumhorns. GDR label Amiga put two albums out before the Berlin wall came down. The five piece are still at it. And if you think the guy on the left looks very much like guitarist Ritchie Blackmore (who likes to dabble in this music himself) then you'd be right, he *does* look very much like Ritchie Blackmore!

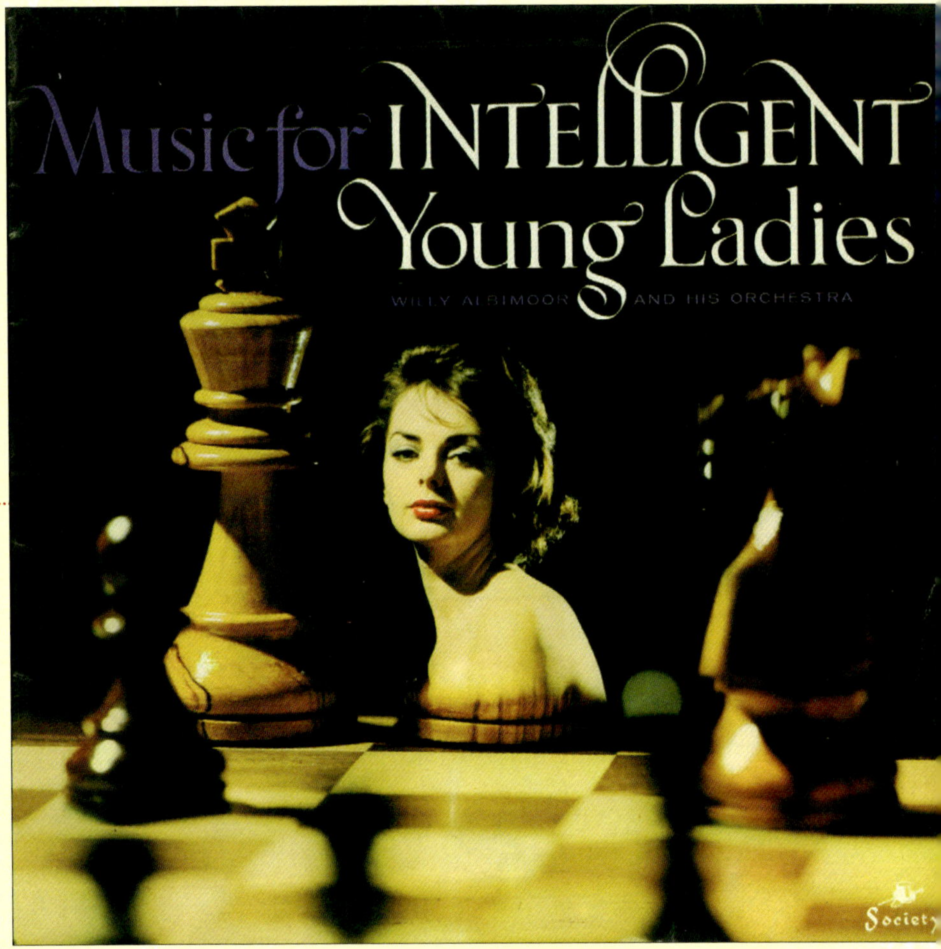

### Willy Albimoor And His Orchestra • Music For Intelligent Young Ladies
Society / UK / 1963 (reissue)

Ladies. Fed up with your husband blowing the food budget on jazz records? Now, as long as you show us your Mensa membership card, you can also treat yourself. And what do you imagine the music might be given the title? If you said *"a fast xylophone-driven instrumental cover of With A Little Bit Of Luck from My Fair Lady"* you would be spot on. Society was a British very budget label of the Fifties and Sixties, sourcing cheap catalogue across Europe, much of which was totally obscure. Willy Albimoor was a Belgian musician, band leader and composer who mostly made his living playing live and appeared on just two albums, of which this - thanks to that astonishing title - is one of the most patronising covers we've ever seen. Making the woman into a chess piece adds sexism to the mix as well. Design wise it is far too sophisticated (!) for Society to have come up with and has a look of Fifties' American design about it, but if it did come out there first we can't find it. The *Music For...* concept was huge in the Fifties. *Music For Expectant Fathers, Music For Frustrated Conductors, Music For Helping You Sleep, Music For Reading*, etc., and the two examples here (right). *"The beat is constantly ingratiating (with) a lilt that could even put a smile of content of the photograph set,"* according to one of the sleeve notes, which hints at a non-English origin and suggests this was long before internet translators were invented.

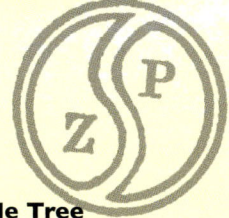

### Trevor Dandy • Don't Cry Little Tree
Zaza Sound / Canada / 1970
*Photographer Lennox Lennard*

We're not fond of vinyl reissues at Easy On The Eye. So many are poorly done as labels crawl over each other to get them onto the market before the bubble bursts. So I did think to see if we could source an original of this, until we discovered it would cost us the best part of £300. However we did source a decent scan, which saves us using the PMG Audio reissue from 2016.
While we understand the photo's eco concept, the sleeve just ended up looking very fey indeed. And it's a ridiculously literal interpretation of the title. Trevor had emigrated to Canada in the Sixties and cut this obscure gospel-funk LP for a local label in 1970. The title track got discovered by the break beat hunters in the early 2000s hence the original becoming so sought after.
Label owner Paul J. Zaza explained it was pressed up in a run of 2,000 for sale to Dandy's church congregation before there was a falling out; *"He had a beef with the church and they basically excommunicated him, and so most of those records ended up in my father's garage. Fast forward to the eighties and I have to clean out the place. I had all these boxes of records, so I just dumped them in a dumpster."* Nobody knows what happened to Trevor who disappeared around the time his overstock hit the skip.
The reissue scanned an original but unable to source the original decorative typeface (it's called Ringlet and was designed in 1882, give us a call next time), they dropped in something approximating it which is why we have not used it.

### Santa Esmeralda • Beauty
Philips / France / 1978
*Photography and cover art Studio de L'Air, Paris*

With make-up straight off the Carry On Screaming film set, this American / French disco outfit earned over 40 platinum award discs by adding drum synths to covers of Sixties' classics. So if a 16 minute version of *House Of The Rising Sun* by The Animals. sounds up your street you know what to search for.
Mostly Santa Esmeralda's sleeve persona rested on glamorous women in vaguely gypsy style costume draping themselves over swarthy guys. Here on their second album we think it's lead singer Jimmy Goings under the short and curlies; by the back cover he's all unbuttoned shirt and finger nail scars across his chest. Studio de L'Air did a lot of excellent sleeve portrait work for French labels from the mid-Seventies on, specialising in high contrast night-time images shot with heavy flash and nicely cropped. So I guess they can be excused this rare turkey, and who knows where the idea came from.

**WILD THING**

**OLD LADY**
b/w Next To Me

VRN 34097
STEREO
Suonabile anche su giradischi mono

Vedette records

# MOTORBIKIN'

**Wild Thing • Old Lady**
Vedette Records / Italy / 1969 7" single

For once WTF is perhaps the only thing to say here. Signed (devised is probably a better word) to / by Elektra in America, this garage / psych band went full-on hair product on the Italian sleeve of this single from their second and last album, where they appeared in chopper / motorcycle mode front and back. Though how they got helmets over that lot is anyone's guess. The group were put together in an attempt to cash-in on the Easy Rider scene, with their first album being all heavy covers of Steppenwolf and the like. We're not sure how this look would have gone down with real bikers at the time mind you (and wouldn't have fancied their chances at Altamont) but it just looks so gloriously mad today. Alvin Stardust would have been very jealous. Here's one of the label's promo photos...

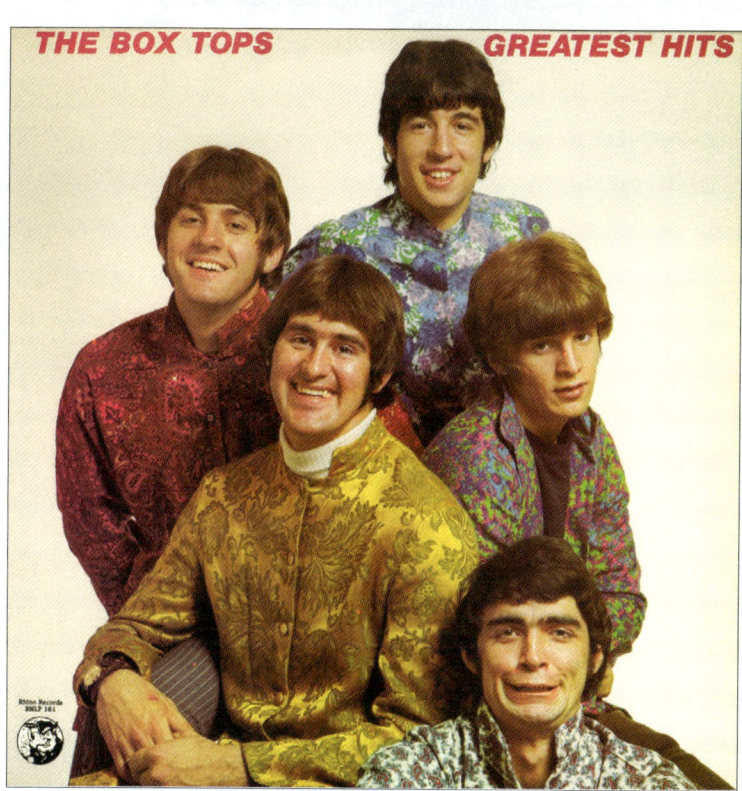

**The Box Tops • Greatest Hits**
Rhino Records / USA / 1982
*Album design Art D. Rekshun*

The Box Tops were not exactly a camera shy band, so why when putting this 'best of' together did Rhino pick the out-take where bassist Gary Talley is gurning like an idiot at the camera? Most bands liked to lark around a little during these otherwise rather boring occasions, but the record label generally put a cross through any

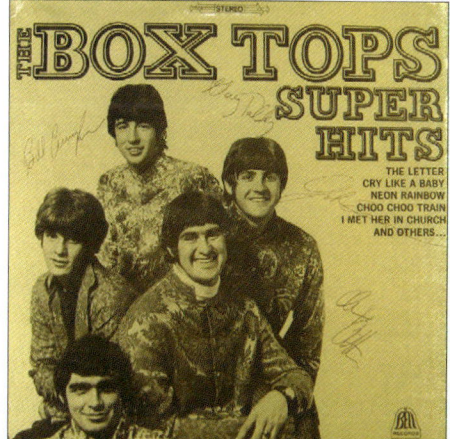

shots they didn't want using on the contact sheet. One explanation here is that Rhino simply couldn't be bothered (the name of the designer suggests they were treating this as a joke) and picked the first colour image they came across at the picture agency. The vintage *Super Hits* (left) shows a more sensible shot from the same photo session.

# Barbara Cartland's Album of Love Songs

## Sung especially for you

# PINK

### Barbara Cartland • Album Of Love Songs
Monza Records / UK / 1978

Before there was Pink, there was PINK. Not many people have the idea of starting a recording career when knocking on 70. I have no idea who thought this would be wise, except as Barbara was the UK's biggest seller of romantic fiction (penning more than 700 books), if everyone who read them also bought an album, then there was a profit to be had somewhere.

No expense was spared; Abbey Road was hired, Norman Newell produced (he did all the top UK solo singers such as Shirley Bassey) and the cover was painted in the style of one of her novels (below). Backing help came from The Royal Philharmonic Orchestra and The Mike Sammes Singers. A lot of help. Barbara wanted to sing, but clearly couldn't! Each song is topped and tailed by self-penned spoken soliloquies. Two years later, she licensed it to another label, and penned a note on the back explaining that the original album must have been too expensive for her admirers as nobody had bought it, so here it was, reissued in pink (her favourite colour) with Barbara at her glamorous best on the front and at an affordable price. Monza (this was their only LP) are probably still sat on a garage full even now.

### Lollipop & The Sprinklers • Candy Man
Pickwick / USA / 1973
*Artwork + collage / Frank Daniel*

This makes your teeth ache just looking at it. The *only* album by Lollipop & The Sprinklers, session players, on a collection of songs relating to sugar, confectionary and sweet food. Daniel did many varied and sometimes excellent covers but on children's records the bar was set rather lower. Mind you if it's pink we're after, what would Cartland make of Doja Cat's 2019 second album (right)?

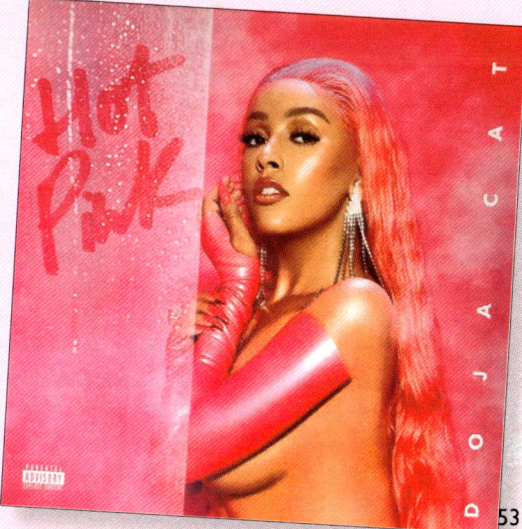

# FREE ALBUMS ON HIFIRECORD'S GET-RICH-PLAN

Increase your profits by 20%. 2 albums free with every purchase of 10 HIFI albums (e.g. $50.00 minimum dealer order must include 1 each of new releases). The entire HIFI album catalog is available for purchase on this plan.

**TABOO VOL. 2**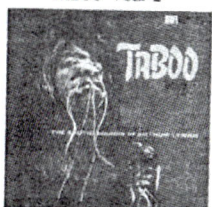
The exotic sounds of Arthur Lyman
HIFIRECORD #822

**SOMETHING BLUE**
The Paul Horn Quintet
HIFIJAZZ #615

**DUTCH BAND ORGAN**
A Dutch import sound novelty
HIFIRECORD #902

### 30 DAYS LEFT ... PLAN ENDS APRIL 30

Order today from your local distributor; or write, wire or phone
HIFIRECORDS, 7803 Sunset Boulevard, Hollywood 46, California
HOllywood 4-4143
"The Sound That Named a Company"

**Arthur Lyman • Taboo Vol. 2**
Vocalion / UK / 1960

Subtitled the *New Exotic Sounds Of Arthur Lyman*, this album rode the wave of what later became known as Easy Listening Lounge music, known amongst vinyl collectors as Exotica. Hawaiian born Lyman is one of the musicians credited with creating this musical genre. Across his thirty albums, designers tried to conjure up the musical mystique with images of tropical islands, exotic beaches and active volcanoes (no fewer than four covers featured those). Taboo sold zillions, so *Vol 2* was a no-brainer. But who decided on what may or may not be a genuine shrunken head (eating spaghetti) for the cover isn't known, nobody was willing to take credit. But it is a truly gruesome sleeve and difficult to see how anyone thought it might sell the album. It certainly doesn't conjure up Hawaii and caused enough fuss in America for HiFi Records to quickly reissue it (top left) with (you guessed it) another volcano picture, copied off Volume 1. It was either that or Lyman trying to look moody as here on *Love For Sale*!

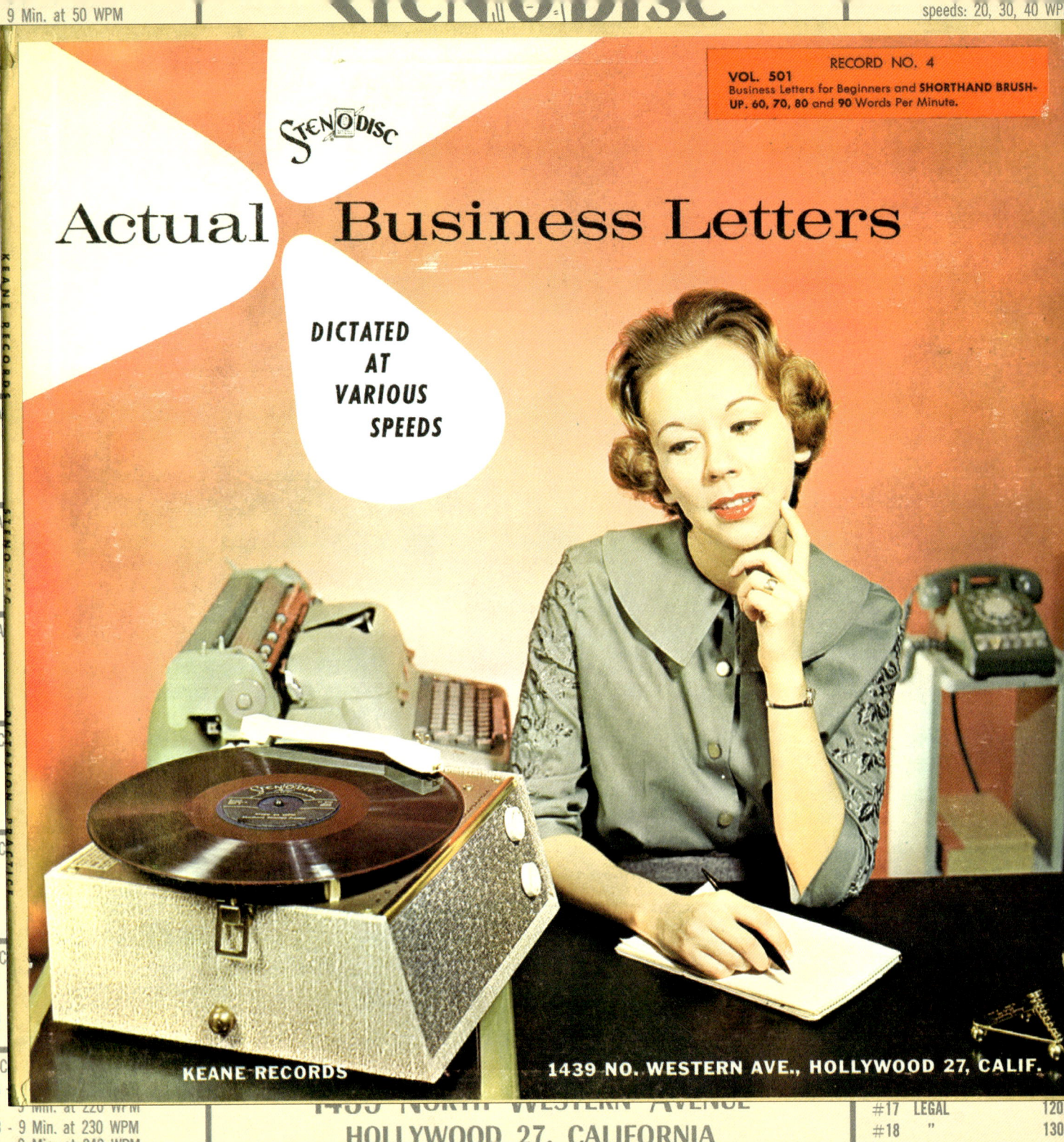

# 80 WORDS PER MINUTE

### Spoken Word • Actual Business Letters
Keane Records Stenodisc / USA / 195-?

Who needs the new Herman's Hermits album when you can spend your hard earned typist's dollars on this? It is a serious business tool, dictating letters for you to transcribe in shorthand. The speed of dictation builds up over two sides as you struggle to keep up. By the end of side two, only your dog will be able to hear it. Keane offered over a dozen of these LPs, all of which have the same cover photo with a sticker on to identify the content (although none instructed you how to deal with over-familiar bosses, probably more of a worry back then). There were also 45s for the more frugal budget. Our cover lady looks like she's working out how to sneak the record player from the office come five o'clock, rather than practising her shorthand. She has been identified as actress and comedienne Carol Burnett, so the label got real value for money out of it. For younger readers, that's a typewriter on the right, a telephone to her left and a fancy pen holder on the desk.

This type of instructional albums were widespread and offer enough remarkably dull sleeves to fill a book on their own. There are more (detailed below) shown on the next page, try and stay awake. If you can think of a tuition idea almost certainly there was an album about it. And we mean *anything*, though we have refrained from showing the blow-job instructional record. A ten inch. I remember having an EP with the multiplication tables set to music to help with my maths. It didn't, but was pressed on snazzy blue vinyl, so may have set me off on the record collecting trail instead.

### How To Communicate Your Ideas
An 'Execudisc' offering *"sound advice on everyday human problems in business"*. It's tempting to buy a copy for our current prime minister (your guess is as good as ours), but as it was *"designed by experts"* I assume she or he will not be interested.

### Norm Hart • The Fascination Of Coins
Undated but produced by Sound Inc in Michigan, the catalogue number suggests mid-1970s but it looks much, much older. Norm drones on for two sides, with track 5 *Commemorative & Fractional Currency* looking particularly helpful for insomniacs.

### Father John Doe • Beyond Sobriety
Produced by RCA's custom records department for the SMT Guild in Indianapolis, these talks were recorded in the late 1940s but could still be ordered in the early 1970s. Astonishingly it is a five LP box set. Frankly, having to plough through all that is more likely to turn you to drink. Father 'John Doe' suggests the speaker wanted to remain anonymous and he turned out at least *thirty* albums, sold individually or in sets.

Disc 10, *Father John Doe - Alcoholic*, does explain why he wanted to keep his name off it. It's the communion wine cellar that was his downfall. If you could still focus after all that drink, there were tie-in books to buy as well.

### W.D. Hlad • Plant Problems Answered
From Hadco Enterprises in 1976, there is a whole side devoted to *Watering And Lighting*. Which is twenty minute longer than they devoted to the sleeve. I like butterflies as much as anyone, but maybe a photo of some plants might have been more to the point?

### How To Become A Better Reader And S-P-E-L-L-E-R
The way they print out the word speller on the cover is priceless, though poor old Johnny looks like he needs lessons in working his record player before he progresses to spelling. Produced by the Palomar Institute, who appear not to have ventured into the vinyl education market ever again.

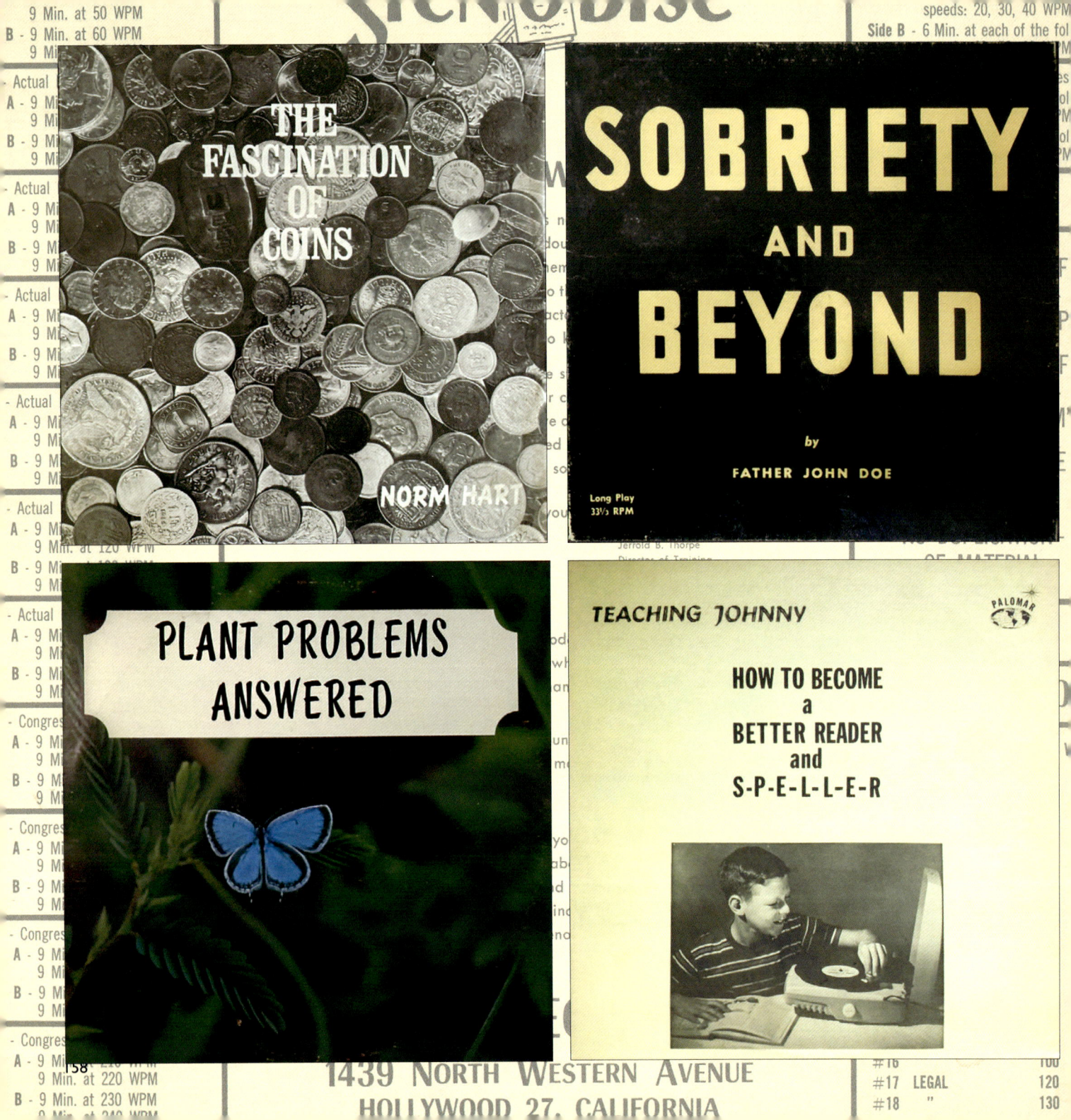

### The World Of • Joseph Cooper
Decca / UK / 1974
*Photograph John Thomson*

Decca's *World Of* series began in 1969, aimed at the middle class market, people who didn't like long haired pop but wanted to show off their stereo with mid-price MOR albums. Joseph Cooper, star of middle-brow BBC 2 TV music quiz Face The Music, which had been running since 1966 (even longer on the wireless), fitted their budget catalogue perfectly. On TV, Cooper bashed away at a silent keyboard, and guests from the classical music world tried to guess from the thumping noise and watching his fingers what he was playing. Well, it was either that or the Black & White Minstrel Show on BBC 1 (and we're not going near *those* infamous covers!). As the dummy keyboard was Cooper's u.s.p the LP cover saw him plonked in a rustic garden plinking away merrily. At least it wasn't going to annoy the neighbours. It does look rather as if Mr Cooper had passed away, stuffed and mounted by his family in the garden as a memento mori, the leaves swept off each spring.
As for the album we *assume* Mr. C switched to a real keyboard for the recording! Decca must have been pleased with sales as a second *World Of* followed, Joseph this time dragging his grand piano out onto the lawn, and then a third volume, where he was allowed back inside, so his rupture could heal. Silliness aside, Cooper was an accomplished pianist, with a vinyl career going back to the late 1950s albeit mostly on budget labels like WRC (above).

### V/A • Future Star Explosion • New Faces Of The 70's
Ember Records / UK / 1970

Ember issued six albums in their Explosion series, each with a dozen or so pop tracks of the era under a theme. The sleeves were generally female models from agency libraries, but for this one they went for the horror film look and a genuinely disturbing double exposure. Indeed I picked it up fully expecting it to be a soundtrack album. It is technically very well done too, unlike some double exposure covers in this book, but as far from K-Tel's 20 Chart Hits as it's possible to go.
We also like the way the label saved money on the Country Explosion collections in the series too (below). When a follow-up seemed a good idea commercially, they simply flipped the cover photo over. Nice to know Ember held their record buyers in such high esteem! Do we think they volunteered a repeat fee to the photo library?

### Sandwich • Kookie
CBS / Germany / 1971

Someone at CBS took the band's (rather limp) name a little too literally on this lacklustre sleeve. A Cologne based rock group, I bet they never expected this group photo to end up being montaged onto a ham sarnie. Possibly hampered by singing in a Cologne dialect (so why print your song titles in English?), they split in 1974.

**Dawn • Tuneweaving**
Bell / USA / 1973
*Cover art Miriam Greenfield. Album design Kaleidoscope. Photography Joel Brodsky. Art direction Beverly Weinstein.*

Yes, this is the album which introduced their massive hit *Tie A Yellow Ribbon Round The Ole Oak Tree* to the world (bet you cannot not play it in your head now). What amazes us here is that four people worked on this gatefold sleeve and at no stage did any of them venture to say *"hey people, this isn't really cutting it, is it?"* Instead they decided to reproduce it larger than life size! On the back sleeve was the original snap (by Joel Brodsky, who did literally hundreds of sleeve photographs). The preliminary sketch on a piece of tapestry, photographed with some reels of cotton (right) is already pointing up the shortcomings of the idea, and might have made a better cover as it was. But by the time it was finished, it was too late to call it in. Though Bell in Australia risked the wrath of Tony Orlando by going with the original colour photo instead (above).

**V/A • Hot Ladies Of Rock**
Pickwick Records / UK / 1982

This is how Pickwick went about presenting their collection of female pop and rock singers, although most of the singers on it would reasonably resent being called a 'hot lady of rock'. As with all things Pickwick it's a bit of a mess, from the unfinished face painting to the awful typography. I wonder whether Tracy Ullman ever did any modelling work early doors, it does look like her...

# OVER WROUGHT IRON

### Big Tom & The Mainliners • The Image Of Me
Denver Records / Eire / 1973
*Photographed by John A McCabe*

*"Front cover shows Big Tom outside his home,"* adds the note on the back helpfully. They also explain that Big Tom McBride's success is "unsurpassed", though it's the first we've heard of him. Having studied this strange image, it seems to be just two photographs montaged together, creating a jumble of shapes, brown suits (yes they were a thing), Toms big and small, plus plenty of (over) wrought iron work. We also wonder who sketched that bizarre guitar shape for the gates? It looks like something Homer Simpson might draw if he'd got a job with Fender. Some might question the wisdom of announcing your success like this to any passing burglar (we even get a look at his trophy room on *Souvenirs*, below). Mind you, if I was breaking in, it would be for those Chelsea boots. Denver Records from Eire catered for the big Irish Country music scene in the Sixties and Seventies with dozens of similar records.

And the sticker? Anyone who has spent time crate digging in Music & Tape Exchange will recognise their famous red countdown label, part of this LPs history. Albums are priced up and racked out, with the price reduced incrementally until it sells. Those with a strong resolve can gamble on saving some money by returning later, but risk finding it has sold.

### The Partridge Family • The Partridge Family Notebook
Bell / USA / 1972
*Design The Music Agency. Art Direction Beverly Weinstein*

The Partridge Family, an American television series from the early Seventies, centred on a widowed mother and her five children who together form a group of the same name. Naturally a slew of tie-in albums (eight in four years, strike while the iron is hot) followed, featuring mostly session players but actor David Cassidy also got involved and then spun off a massive solo career. The album covers (all done by The Music Agency who worked mostly for the Bell label) were designed to relate to teenagers lives, so *Sound Magazine* looked like a teen magazine cover, while *Shopping Bag* contained an actual plastic bag inside (I've still never found one!). *Notebook* (above) must have taken minutes to brainstorm, just a sheet of punched lined excercise paper, which might have sounded like a good idea but ended up as one of the dullest sleeves of all time. So dull that in the UK and elsewhere they added a snapshot of the family (and in Japan they ran a colour photo across the whole front). (Right) Even in America Bell later changed the design!

# TOP HIT AUS HOLLAND

**Mistral • Jamie / Nectar**
CNR / Holland / 1977

A studio only Dutch synth pop band, featuring female vocalists and musicians (from Shocking Blue and Ekseption) who should have known better. Still it's kind of reassuring to know that for every awful act we in the UK endured on Top Of The Pops, viewers in Holland and across Europe were suffering even more. Though whether their outfits were dafter than those of The Spotniks a decade or more earlier is hard to know.
Dressing up like insects and getting a hit single, their TV promo for this their debut 7" featured clips of mating insects and quickly had the Dutch equivalent of Mary Whitehouse (that cannot have been an easy job) reaching for the posh notepaper to complain. Once it went Top 10, France and Germany piled in, using alternate shots below which (despite the less than great scan of the Dutch sleeve) together give us the full dreadful scope of the photo shoot.
Mind you their contributions to sci-fi art also leave a lot to be desired, Starship 109 (right) is regularly treasured by worst sleeve curators online. Mistral later lost the plot completely for *You're My Hero* in 1980 (see the start of this book) which saw their chart career come to an end.

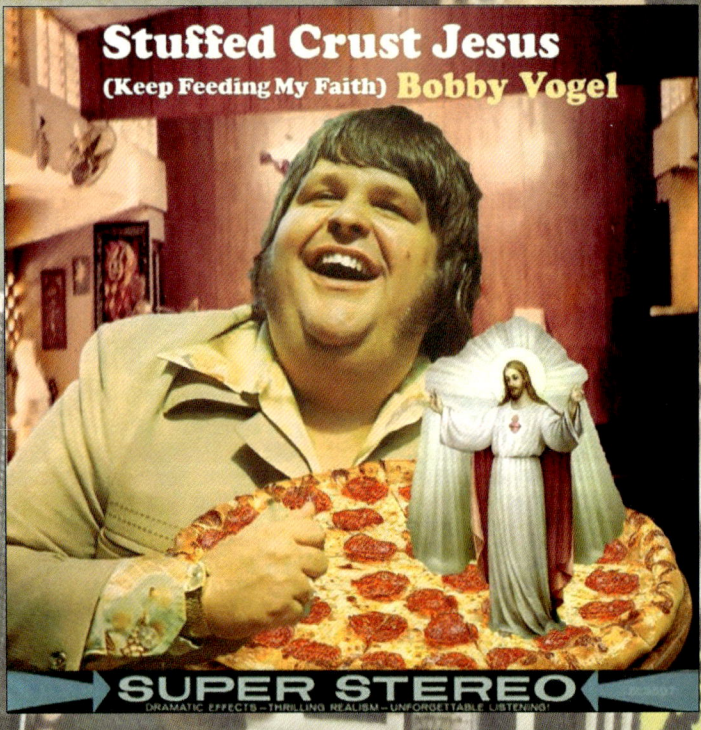

# IS IT MEMOREX?

## WHIPPED CREAM

While on the lookout for strange album covers, Steve soon encountered the world of fake album sleeves. Some people enjoy putting their own twist on existing front covers. Once posted on the web, these memes get picked up and without bothering to check, many end up in "worst records" galleries across the internet. Here are two Steve came across, along with the original covers which we thought it would be fun to show as examples of the genre.

Country and Western singer **"Little" David Wilkins** issued *King Of All The Taverns* in 1976 on MCA which probably deserves a place in Steve's collection anyway. This sleeve then inspired *Stuffed Crust Jesus*, a montage which is widely included as a genuine cover on many lists and a cut up almost worthy of Richard Hamilton, though the prankster remains unknown.

Another cover which would probably have made this book had we been able to find a copy is *Accordeonpourri*, by accordion duo **De Kermisklanten**. Issued in 1973, their hair styles astonish on dozens of albums, on which they rattle through pop hits of the day. The coiffure remains here on the otherwise much doctored space-aliens deviant art take on the cover. Again this appears all over the web, possibly painted by someone directly onto a sleeve as the work is very convincing, though our attempts to trace them for a credit so far have been in vain.

### Various • Salad Days • The Boy Friend
World Record Club / UK / Jul 1962

Both these stage musicals began life in the Fifties and spawned any number of versions, two of which were paired on this release by the mail-order only World Record Club. WRC often used simple, clever and unadorned images on their albums (rarely credited) as they stood out better in the catalogues. Here though, in what looks like the antithesis of design, they took things to the literal limit with what looks to be a slide from a greengrocer's sales leaflet. Goodness knows what they would have used had the label led with The Boyfriend. Easily one of the most deadly dull covers in this book, the album was issued at the time stereo was beginning to take off, hence the sticker (a mono press was also issued). Format wars are nothing new.

 Back in the real world, Trumpeter Herb Alpert founded A&M in the early Sixties, and for his fourth album went with a design by our old faves, Peter Whorf Graphics. *Whipped Cream & Other Delights* (above) sold 6 million copies and back in 1965 was seriously saucy stuff, rightly becoming a favourite of sleeve collectors. It has also inspired a lot of tributes, some of which are very bizarre. Here are four of the worst!

### The Frivolous Five • Sour Cream & Other Delights
RCA Victor / USA / 1966

Nobody wanted to take credit for this Tijuana-flavoured, Herb Alpert-esque pop pastiche. Little is known about the musical comedy quintet responsible either, signed by RCA after a US TV talent show. Stockists of shaving foam must have rubbed their hands after this order came through.

### Pat Cooper • Spaghetti Sauce & Other Delights
United Artists / USA / 1967
*Artwork Frank Gauna*

One side of spoken comedy and one side of song parodies, and cover-wise reminds us of The Who's notorious *Sell Out* album.

### Soul Asylum • Clam Dip & Other Delights
Twin Tone Records / 1988.
*Swiped Graphics by Dan Kalal*

I hate to think what the photo studio was like after this had been under the lighting for a couple of hours.

### Various Artists • Right To Chews - Bubblegum Classics Revisited
Not Lame / 2002
*Artwork Mike Simmons (Photo Peter Kuehl)*

An album of power pop remakes of 60s classics let down by a fairly tatty attempt at covering the model in gum. It's a blanket. We can all see it's a blanket.

### Peter Rabbitt • Roadstar
AVI Records / USA / 1979
*Design Foxworthy Graphics Photography Kenneth Shearer*

*"Mixed using the Peter Rabbitt Oral Exciter"*. As noted in his intro, this was the album which set Steve off, and it is enough to give you mixamatosis just looking at it. The group seem to have been from Southern California (their 'fan club' was located in La Jolla), but otherwise Peter Rabbitt are something of a mystery, with no names on the sleeve beyond successful songwriter and producer Douglas LA Foxworthy. Was this his own band? Taking their musical cues from MOR acts like Styx and Foreigner, they weren't bad on disc, or live, say people who saw them. But it's the mad, nightmarish cover which fascinates us. Like other animal / human hybrid sleeves in the book it provokes varied reactions when seen for the first time. Just ask Steve! Rabbitt were an early signing to AVI Records who had faith in the material, with a repackaged LP a couple of years later, and a unique promotion-only cover as well (both above right, one very worn!), both possibly out-takes from the original shoot. Now very rare, though if you picked a handful of copies up at the $2.98 discount price shown, you could turn a decent profit today.

### Holograf • Stai În Poala Mea
Electrecord / Romania / 1995 CD / LP / cassette
*Coperta Iulian Vrabete, Radu Leonte. Photography Cornel Ugly God David, George Chelmec*

That another outfit would work with rabbits seems hard to believe but Romanian rockers Holograf did just that on this arena rock comeback LP. Formed in 1977 and very successful in the country, they had a few years away in the Nineties trying to make it abroad, returning with this album, Sit On My Lap. Exactly what inspired them to pose with nothing but a rabbit each to cover their modesty must remain buried in Romanian folklore, as the band, having mellowed into a soft rock outfit after this (or forgotten to trim the rabbit's claws), stopped updating their website / playing live a few years ago. The provocative image got them onto the front page of the newspapers and has bemused strange sleeve collectors ever since. Look for the out-take photo on the cassette edition if you holiday in Romania!

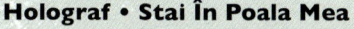

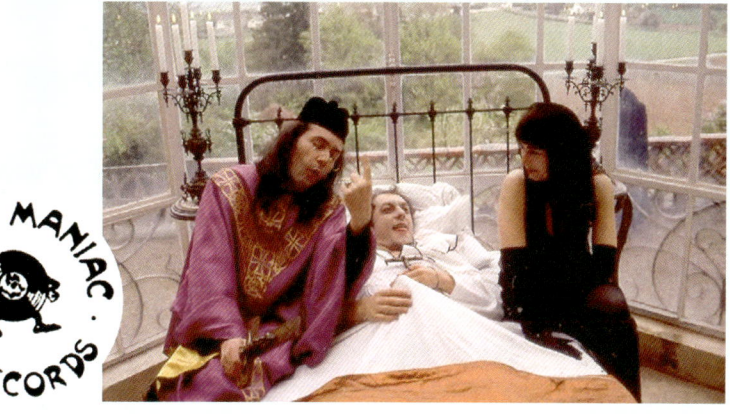
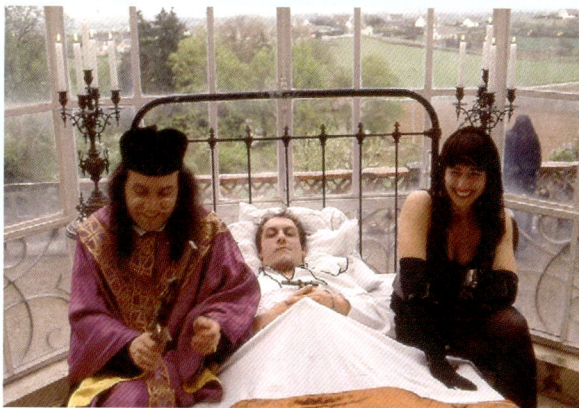

### Vietnam Chain • Before I Go
Music Maniac Records / Germany / 1989 12" single

Well there is certainly something rising from the dead here but Ingrid Pitt never faced anything quite like this in the films. Formed as a one album side project by garage bands from Germany (Daisy Chain) and France (Vietnam Veterans), this was the strangely attired single off the LP. The photograph is not credited (I think it was by singer / guitarist Mark Enbatta) but is from the album cover sessions (out-takes above) and has everything a bizarre sleeve could want; a mad priest, a grieving widow and a Rik Mayall look-a-like having problems keeping his bed sheets on. Outside, death beckons. It is generally high on people's poll listings at Steve's exhibition! It's not a bad single, with great female vocals, if low production values. The Vietnam Veterans soldiered on well into the 2000s but Mark died in 2021.

### Duduca & Dalvan • Massa Falida
Gel Records / Brazil
*Foto Walmir T Silva. Capa WOM Publicidade*

Emerging from the water like some nightmarish aquatic Dr. Who invaders from the planet Tie-Rack, Duduca & Dalvan took Brazilian country music airwaves by storm in the 1980s and indeed continue to work, albeit with a new Duduca (the original died in 1986). We have no idea what the angel was all about; some farcical aquatic ceremony?

**BRISTOL HOTEL KEMPINSKI**

# Im KEMPINSKI Grill

# Good Time Music

**Hellmuth Schindler • Im Kempinski Grill**
Exquisit / Germany / 1960 (?)

Hellmuth, resident piano and organ player at the Bristol Hotel's Kempinski restaurant in Berlin during the Sixties, runs through his repertoire of 30 cheesy riffs lifted from various classical pieces. The Bristol was the one and only luxury hotel in the city when it opened in 1951, and somebody hit on the idea of promoting the place with this album (and single), probably sold as souvenirs. Now I don't know about you, but if I were promoting my restaurant I would tend to photograph it on a busy evening to give everybody the idea of how popular it was. Not Herr Kempinski, who has chosen a Marie Celeste-like shot instead, surely be one of the blandest sleeves of all time. Phonocolor Schallplatten GmbH were a manufacturer of privately pressed records and flexi-discs in Berlin under the Exquist and other names. The hotel is still going strong by the way, though sadly has lost all the cool Sixties fixtures and fittings.

**Various • Good Time Music**
Imperial House / Canada / 1977 3LP
*Jacker Bill Hicks Design*

Should that not be *30 Dad Dancing Greats*? As woeful a quartet of unconvincing ravers as we will ever see on a record sleeve. How does that song at the end of Blazing Saddles go? *Throw out your hands, Stick out your tush, Hands on your hips Give them a push...*

Otherwise the frogs will be coming for you...

**The Erwins • One More Night With The Frogs**
Rainbow Records / USA / 1980
*Art design The Erwins. Cover photo Mr Lynn M Stone*

I was sure this was another faked sleeve but happily (for us) it turns out to be genuine. Yet again the Lord has inspired this, via the Dennis K. Erwin Evangelistic Association in Texas. Anyway, there is method in the cover madness, a reference to God's plague of frogs. *"We pray these songs will bring joy to all who hear them,"* The Erwins write on the back. If they don't, remember those frogs and start dancing. Oh, and a big thanks *"to my Dad, for his sacrificial help."* Perhaps best not to ask what that involved. The Erwins seem to have been a band, with Dennis's stepmother involved. He later married Tiffany and they have since spawned a quartet of younger Erwins, *"proving the future of Southern Gospel music is secure."* Thank goodness.

# INTRODUCTION AND INNER COVERS

**The Faith Tones • Jesus Use Me**
Angelus Records / USA / 1964 [inside cover]

Possibly one of the most cherished 'worst sleeves' of all time, a $300 price tag today. On the left is Matthew Broderick, a chubby-cheeked Justin Bieber in the middle and on the right a young Stephen Fry.

**Dr. Murray Banks • How To Quit Smoking**
Murmil Associates / USA / 1965 [inside cover]

I think most people would rather carry on than have to listen to this.

**A Los Wankas • Dile Si!**
Discos Prodisar/ 1986 / Peru [inside cover]

Stop sniggering. You have heard of the Incas. The Wankas are another Peruvian tribe, inspiring a world music quintet, and causing hilarity everywhere else.

**Mary McCaslin • Old Friends**
Philo / USA / 1977 [inside cover]
Margot Zalkind-Schur Design. Photography Norman Seeff

Cover the moustache and nose hairs up … and it's a great sleeve.

**Gary • Getting Down To Business**
Sound Shop Records / USA / 1978 [page 5]

Dr. Gary Solomon, nowadays running a cinematherapist treatment service, responds to the photographer's instructions to *"make love to the camera"*. Is that a cheque book down his trousers or is he just pleased to have a solo album out? Recorded in Nashville, Gary opened for the Pistols on their infamous US tour. Only kidding.

**Red Simpson • I'm A Truck**
Capitol / USA / 1972 [page 1]
John Hoernle Art Direction, Roy Kohara Design

To say Red was obsessed with trucks is an understatment. Hence *Hello, I'm A Truck*, featuring *I'm A Truck*, *Drugstore Truck Driver*, *Good Old Truckin' Girl*, *Truckin' Man*, *I Just Kept On Trucking* and many many more. Great cover photo, but the title cracks me up every time. Steve allowed it in to shut me up I think.

**Ray Franky • Ik Dank Je**
Hebra Records / Belgium / 1987 [page 180]

Maybe Mr. Musk would like to explain how Franky, born 1917, regularly update his blue badge Twitter account twenty years after his death? Ray was 70 when he posed for this scary looking photo, having issued his first 78 back in 1951. The question is why would you pluck up the courage to go to a wig shop, then pick this one? He also recorded as Ray Franky En Zijn Hoempa Zangers, which sounds so rude we're not even going to run it through a translator in case it lets us down. Let's hope Record Day Belgium gets around to reissuing this soon.

**Miss Piggy's • Aerobique**
Warner Bros / Henson Universal Music / USA / 1982
Design Diana Zadarla Photography John E. Barrett

[right] Steve was at one of his exhibitions when two medical emergency staff arrived to some consternation. They pulled this out of a charity shop bag, and thought it might be a decent addition to the show. They weren't wrong! It is one of those albums which is disturbing on a number of levels, yet at the same time very funny when you read the cover in detail. They must have had a great fun putting it together, complete with a fsheet of dubious exercises. And remember, 'an empty stomach is the devil's trolley car.'

**Jerry LaCroix • The Second Coming**
Phonogram / USA / 1974 [page 5]
Art direction, design and illustration Richard Mantell. Cover co-ordination Jeanne Sasaki for AGI.

Yo! Rock, Blues, Folk, World AND Country, according to one review. But as Jerry worked with Edgar Winter's White Trash, Blood, Sweat & Tears *and* Rare Earth, you begin to get some idea of his talents. This was the second of only two solo albums where he suddenly went all half-man half-lion on us (except in South Africa where they went with the photo off the back instead). Mantell's sleeve work is extensive and generally second to none but this one does neither Jerry or lions any favours!

**Terry Gilmore • Terry**
Gilmore Productions / USA / ? [page 180]

Another self-pressed gospel gem. Terry had three goes at a self portrait, couldn't decide which was the best, so treated us to them all. Cheers.

**Skeff • Panpan Kuku**
Splendid Music / France / 1977 7" single [inside back]
Photo Rene Ona, Maquette David Ducros

The Profanosaurus dictionary of rude phrases has an entry: "The French were involved". Meaning: something has gone horribly wrong. If they ever do an illustrated edition, they need look no further than this sleeve to demonstrate the phrase.

**Mistral • You're My Hero**
Polydor / Germany [page 6] (see page 166 for more costume nightmare covers by this duo)

**Locomotiv GT III • Bummm!**
Pepita / Hungary /1973 [inside back]
Grafika Kemény György

… although Robert Crumb probably has as much right to the honours. Hungarian prog rockers fourth album gets lost in translation! The illustration continues on the back of the gatefold, but doesn't get any better.

**Teriyaki Asthma • Vol I - V**
C/Z Records / USA / 1991 [inside back]
D. House Design. Rhonda Pelikan Design. Charles Peterson Photography.

Ten volumes (LPs and EPs), a sort of indie / grunge *Nuggets* for the 90s. Here they let loose with this homage to Prince's narcissism and metal bands. Daniel House (who may even be the cover model), certainly makes an arresting (or arrestable) image while Peterson worked on sleeves for the Sub Pop label.

**Tozovac • Jeremija**
PGP / Yugoslavia / 1972 7" single [inside back]

Tozovac (real name Predrag Živković) was a Serbian folk singer, writer and accordionist (surely Serbia must have other instruments?). Here he phallically straddles a piece of artillery, though despite the look, he was one of the Serbs who had no time for Slobodan Milošević and was not afraid to say so. It took Covid to end his long career at 86.

# EASY ON THE EYE BOOKS • OUT AND ABOUT

More details and to order online direct from us, visit www.easyontheeyebooks.wordpress.com

We are always interested in hearing from collectors who may have ideas for future titles, contact us via the website. We urge customers to support local bookshops. The big online retail tax avoider is crippling small independent publishers, bookshops and specialist retailers (https://www.ethicalconsumer.org/ethicalcampaigns/boycott-amazon). Oh and fuck Brexit. Please.

## OUT NOW

**GRAHAM BONNET • THE AUTHORISED BIOGRAPHY**
The Story Behind The Shades • ISBN: 978 0 9561439 7 6
The career of one of rock's greatest singers, from the clubs of hometown Skegness, to fronting Ritchie Blackmore's Rainbow on Top Of The Pops and headlining Donington. Loads of rare and unseen photos, plus a gig diary, discography and more.

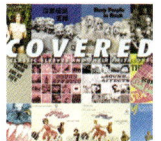

**COVERED! Classic Sleeves And Their Imitators**
ISBN: 978-0-9561439-2-1
The title says it all. 1,000 sleeves shown and annotated; funny, sharp and subversive versions of well known sleeves by bands from around the globe. Very entertaining, and very amusing! If you enjoyed BIZARRE ALBUMS you will love this.

**DEEP PURPLE • WAIT FOR THE RICOCHET**
The Story of Deep Purple In Rock, 1969 - 1970
ISBN : 978-0-9561439-6-9 [Second edition]
The matching title to Fire In The Sky (below). A detailed look at one of the most famous and hard hitting rock albums of all time, profusely illustrated, and very well reviewed by journalists and fans around the world.

## FORTHCOMING and IN THE PIPELINE

**DEEP PURPLE • FIRE IN THE SKY**
The Story of Machine Head and Smoke On The Water
ISBN : 978-0-9561439-9-0 [2024]
Following our acclaimed first book, the story of one of the most successful rock albums and singles of all time. Beset by fire and police raids, the band ended up recording their biggest hits in an empty hotel corridor.

**BOOM BOOM BOOM BOOM** • American Rhythm & Blues 1962 – 66 : The photographs of Brian Smith • ISBN : 978-0-9561439-4-5 [2024]
A fabulous collection of rare and unseen images taken of many Blues greats taken in Manchester in the Sixties by young photographer and Twisted Wheel club regular Brian Smith. From lost negatives and prints, newly scanned for the book, annotated throughout.

**STARSTRUCK** • Art of Japanese Single Sleeve
ISBN: 978-0-9561439-0-7
Japan was one of the first countries to issue vinyl singles in picture sleeves, and were free to do their own covers. This book will present a stunning selection of 7" covers from the 60s to the 80s, around a thousand striking and collectable sleeves in colour.

**WHEN COVER GIRLS RULED THE WORLD**
The Top Of The Pops Albums • ISBN: 978-0-9561439-1-4
Anyone partying in the 70s will remember the Top Of The Pops albums, budget collections with a difference - these were all covers! The story of how the albums came about, the heroic efforts of the session players and of course the famous cover girls. Still in the pipeline.

---

## MUSIC WEEK TOP ALBUMS

**Voted for at the exhibitions! Huddersfield 2021**
1 : Peter Rabbitt • Roadstar Rock n Roll
2 : Carlos • Hier Aujourd'hui
3 : Gerhard Polt • Leberkas Hawaii
4 : Dan Crary • Lady's Fancy
5 : Jim Post • I Love My Life
6 : Yello • Solid Pleasure
7 : Disco do Fofao • 2
8 : Dave McKenna, The Wilbur Little Quartet • Oil and Vinegar
9 : Trevor Dandy • Don't Cry Little Tree
10 : Billy Cobham / George Duke Band • Live on Tour in Europe

Our first chart saw Peter Rabbitt shoot to the top with old time favourites not far behind!

**Spode Museum 2022**
1 : Riot • Narita
2 : Dave McKenna, The Wilbur Little Quartet • Oil and Vinegar
3 : Carlos • Hier Aujourd'hui
4 : Alan Franklin • Come Home Baby
5 : Peter Rabbitt • Roadstar Rock n Roll
6 : Disco do Fofao • 2
7 : The Vietnam Chain • Before I Go
8 : Dan Crary • Lady's Fancy
9 : Jean Pierre Jumez • The Nimble Fingers of
10 : Jim Post • I Love My Life

Riot goes straight in at number one and pushes Peter Rabbitt down to five! Dave McKenna climbs to number two. New entries for Alan Franklin and Jean Pierre Jumez

**Shambala Festival 2022**
1 : Peter Rabbitt • Roadstar Rock n Roll
2 : Disco do Fofao • 2
3 : Dave McKenna, The Wilbur Little Quartet • Oil and Vinegar
4 : Mustard Seed Street Church • May You See Jesus This Christmas
5 : Carlos • Hier Aujourd'hui
6 : The Vietnam Chain • Before I Go
7 : Gerhard Polt • Leberkas Hawaii
8 : Riot • Narita
9 : Alan Franklin • Come Home Baby
10 : Jim Post • I Love My Life

Another new entry for the Mustard Seed Street Church Christmas album, while Peter Rabbitt regains the number one slot. Jim Post still hanging in there at number ten.

**Huddersfield 2023**
1 : Holograf • Stai In Poala Mea
2 : Dave McKenna, The Wilbur Little Quartet • Oil and Vinegar
3 : Carlos • Hier Aujourd'hui
4 : Mustard Seed Street Church • May You See Jesus This Christmas
5 : The Vietnam Chain • Before I Go
6 : Panpan Kuku • Skeff
7 : Gerhard Polt • Leberkas Hawaii
8 : The Faith Tones • Jesus Use Me
9 : Eddie Barclay • Surprise Party!
10 : Riot • Narita

Four new entries this time, including rabbit fondlers Holograf straight in at number one! Riot have dropped to number ten but Eddie Barclay jumps in and becomes one of our oldest chart entries.

# EASY ON THE EYE BOOKS • CREDITS

easy on the eye books / nethergate / sheffield.
www.easyontheeyebooks.wordpress.com
Text and design copyright © Easy On The Eye Books 2023

Artwork, design, print, scanning and image restoration Easy On The Eye. Main book set in adobe gill sans.

First edition 2023. British Library Cataloguing in Publication Data. A catalogue record for this book is available from the British Library.
ISBN 978-0-995-523647

All rights reserved. No part of this publication may be reproduced, stored in a retrieval system, or transmitted, in any form or by any means, electronic, mechanical, photocopying, recording or otherwise, without the prior permission of the publishers.

Original sleeve art remains the copyright of their respective labels and designers who are credited in the text. The majority of the sleeves in this book are from the collection of Steve Goldman (with some additional images from Easy On The Eye). Every attempt has been made to trace designers and copyright owners, we will be happy to credit anyone we have missed in future editions.

STEVE GOLDMAN wishes to thank:
My wife Lorna & children Jenny and Sam - my partners in crime.
My parents Mick and Ann for always believing in me.
The Stroke Team at Calderdale Royal Infirmary, it wouldn't have been possible without you.
All the people who've volunteered at the exhibitions since they started; it wouldn't have been possible without you either.
Richard Byrne, for continuing to provide publicity for the project (and what publicity!).
Michael Escolme at the Spode Museum for organizing the exhibition there, and helping me get more.
Simon Robinson (and Ann) for producing this book.

If you know of a venue that you think would be interested in hosting an exhibition, please get in touch with Steve Goldman (worstrecordcovers@gmail.com). Steve also presents a great website of weird travel and map related stuff (mapfodder.com).

EASY ON THE EYE would like to thank: Steve for trusting us doing his collection proud. All the staff at the Sheffield NHS Teaching Hospital without whom, like Steve, we could literally not have done this either (pay them; what else matters?). Tom Dixon, who first alerted me to Steve's exhibition, and just knew we'd be interested. John Tucker for his interest and proof reading input. Nick and Nick Robinsons for the Easy Shop. Ruth Morrison for her help. Dan Hollingsworth at Star Books. We have visited many websites in researching this book but Discogs.com has been great help in fact checking. Thanks to them and the many collectors who contributed that way.
Lastly, a special thank-you to Stewart Lee for so readily agreeing to do us a foreward and really going to town. He will always be our 41st Best Standup Ever!

LINKS • see the project evolve and get exhibition details at
**instagram.com/worstrecordcovers** and/or **facebook.com/worstrecordcovers**
https://st33.wordpress.com • Simon's website devoted to vinyl sleeve art.
https://easyontheeye2.wordpress.com • Simon's design, photo and retro site.
https://easyontheeyeshop.co.uk • Easy On The Eye Books official online shop.

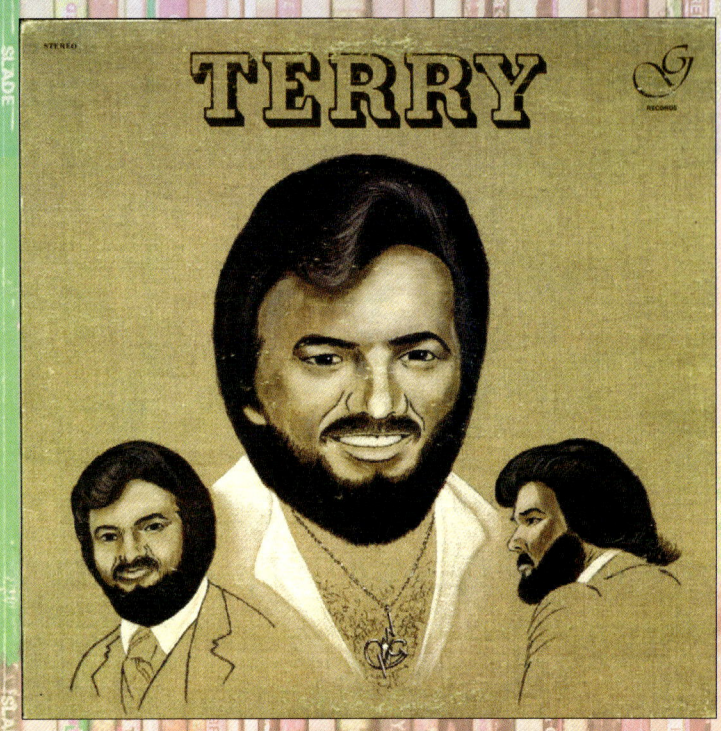